THE WEST GRAND
HAUNTING

BY MICHAEL OKA

The West Grand Haunting

Paperback edition ISBN: 979-8-9851865-7-4
Electronic edition ISBN: 979-8-9851865-8-1

Published by Madhouse Books
Spring Valley, California
http://www.MadhouseBooks.com

First Edition: April 2024

TABLE OF CONTENTS

FORWARD

What I am about to tell you is a true story.

It's not *based* on a true story or an *interpretation* of a true story.

This account—*my firsthand account*—is thirty-four years in the making; thirty-four years to figure out in repetition how *not* to write it, thirty-four years to find a way to tell it from a genuine place.

Thirty-four years of my life peppered in nightmares that were once made manifest to me as a child.

There are so many things that scare a child.

The darkness behind a closet door that *must* be closed by bedtime; the space under the bed checked and cleared before lights out. The bedroom door can't be shut lest the darkness takes an unlucky child into the void. Every child knows these things and understands that blankets are a safe zone. Luckily, moms and dads are there to tuck you in—unless they're not.

For a child, nothing is scarier than a lost parent. No ghost can do to a child what an empty seat at the table can.

...but they can come close.

For Mom and Dad

The West Grand House

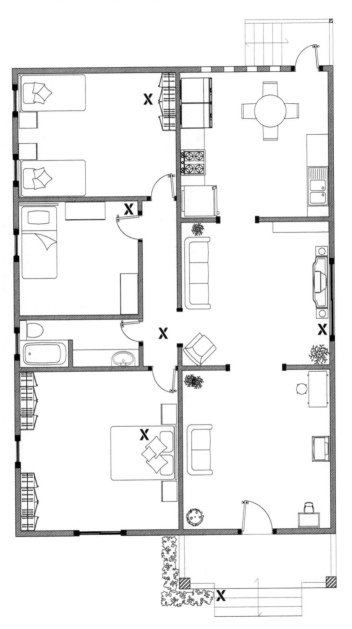

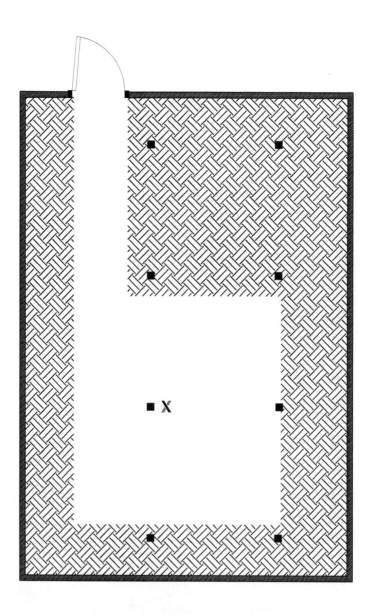

X = Locations of Occurrences

OCTOBER 5, 1988

My father woke me in the early hour just before sunrise on that October morning in 1988, that golden hour whose glow and glory comes only twice a day. I was still in my pajamas when we stepped out, leaving my mom and sister to sleep quietly in bed as Dad locked the door behind us.

The morning air was visibly misty, a thick sheet of fog rolling over the empty boulevard in front of our house there on Grand. There were no sounds; even the birds were silent, still sleeping on their perches or nests. You must understand the *importance* of this moment for me.

Mom and Dad were in the "let's try again' phase after leaving my sister and me as distraught children for nearly two years.

Our desktop computer was, in fact, a heavyset desktop computer with that memorable monochromatic headache-inducing screen that showed a basic font in spinach green. Back then, to get to whatever program we wanted to use, each entry had to begin with "CD" for *Change Directory*. These were the days when the wrong input resulted in a *"bad command or file name"* response. If you were using a Macintosh, it would reply, *"syntax error."*

There were no blogs or online portals to share on social media. Social media was handled in the classroom, passing notes back and forth behind the teacher's back when they weren't looking. Dating apps were a simple piece of paper your crush handed you (or that you handed to your crush) that read:

Do you like me **Y** ☐ **N** ☐ *?*

There was no swiping right or left.

Our world still slept in darkness, and our only information contained whatever was shown on the evening news. Whatever evils existed in the world— there were many—seldom made it to any viral capacity in our self-contained world and isolated lives.

There was a sense of wonder that morning: the mist, the fog, and, for me, the strange smell of a new world. I rarely had a scarce relationship with my dad for two years. At this moment, we boarded his van, which smelled like orange groves mingling with the scent of Brut (Dad's go-to aftershave).

The gray minivan was more of a hybrid cargo van with an illegally installed non-DOT seat bolted into the cargo area. The only window in the back was a rear windshield that stretched the width of the back hatch.

I didn't ask where we were going in what was a comfortably quiet ride along the grand circle. Later in life, I would learn that the road we drove along was once a drag racing track in 1914, but that day, I enjoyed the newness as we cruised along West Grand, turning right on Sixth Street, right again on Rimpau, and finally at the Magnolia cross street, grinning at the surprise of McDonald's for a breakfast stop.

I'll never forget waiting in line in the drive-through (which I hated being spelled as "drive-thru") or ordering two whole sausage biscuits to myself. Dad ordered three pancake breakfasts: one for him, one for my mom, and one for my little sister.

This is my earliest memory of Corona as a younger child. It is the fondest memory of my father and probably the last *truly* good memory I'll have while my parents are still married.

After that, everything would be a slow burn toward a living horror story of the waking physical world, the nightmare-scape of a troubled child, and the brief terror of living in a house that hated our family.

...THE WAY THINGS WERE

I was born on a leap year, on Tuesday, April 29, 1980, in Harbor City, California, Los Angeles. Jimmy Carter was the president of the United States, and Deborah Anne Harry—*Blondie*—shook the airwaves as *Call Me* rose to number one on the charts.

Within a month of my birth, Mount Saint Helens erupted in a cataclysmic event that destroyed Skamania County in Washington state and sent a column of ash so high that the ash surrounded the world *while* creating a hundred and fifty new lakes and ponds. On the evening of December 8th that year, John Lennon was murdered outside his New York City apartment.

Great Grandpa Oka passed away in 1985 after we moved to Lawndale. Grandma Oka followed him to the pearly gates in 1986. Emphysema.

Great Grandpa Oka, who I am told cherished me, exists now only in vague glimpses. An armchair in Grandpa Oka's living room and quaint Japanese snacks ranging from rice crackers wrapped in dried nori to small pieces of dried fish patties are flavors I'll never forget, not simply because I still eat them. All I know is he was there one day, and then suddenly, when I was five, he wasn't there anymore.

I was six when Grandma Oka passed away from emphysema. Dad was devastated, though I never saw it.

Mom told me then that a funeral was no place for a little boy, but Grandma Oka had gone to heaven. That was what death was to me in the early 1980s.

Dad raised me in Catholicism. Mom raised me in faith, a path I would later embrace with open arms. You were either here in the world or with God in heaven.

Back then, I could only count my days with time. I rushed forward with my heart set on Easter break, Summer Vacation, and Christmas break. Back then, that was what we called it.

Back then, that was what it was.

The days were magical. I came home from Anderson Elementary School, changed out of my nice clothes into my play clothes, and I could play outside until the streetlights came on.

Back then, the hidden gears of life turned everywhere. Grandma and Grandpa Denney moved from their home in Redondo Beach to a handsome townhouse in Brea, California. I remember going there with my sister to spend the night shortly after they had settled in. The streetlights on the roads turned from cold white lights to soft yellow streetlights as Grandma said they would. Their Brea home was beautiful.

It was the last month of the summer of 1987 when Mom and Dad split up for their *trial* separation. Dad moved out, and my mom's sister, my Aunt, took over the lease at the house on Freeman Avenue. Mom moved us in with Grandma and Grandpa Denney in Brea. My sister and I powered through our devastation, and when the school year came, we attended Ladera Palma Elementary School.

I had friends in Lawndale, school friends, and neighborhood friends on Freeman Avenue. As tempted as I am to flex the names of every one of them, the details are as inconsequential to the dread building: inconsequential to the story. They were only punctuations of my childhood, ellipses, and exclamations that faded from the paragraphs in the story of my life.

I didn't have those friends in Brea. I was alone. Not alone in my grandparents' home, in the house that felt almost like home, save that it was *not*. My little sister and I attended school. Mom worked and saved money.

The passage of time moved ever forward, through visiting cousins, aunts, and uncles, and into birthdays. It was just at the beginning of the summer of 1988 that my mom, with cautious optimism, began seeing my dad again. He took us to his company store and let us choose whatever we wanted. We went to some fair outside where he was staying. Just after September of 1988, after lots of visiting, Mom announced that Dad was looking for a new home for all of us.

Which brings us back to October 1988—to where it all began.

TOUCHSTONES

Wile you are young, there is a place where you can still reach your lost childhood. A place between those childish things and putting those childish things away. It is a place where innocence is still navigating the concept of growing up, and for my sister and me, that place was the Root Cellar.

There, beneath the house, stored in boxes we had not seen for two years, were our toys—*the best on planet earth*—and those toys carried energy to them.

That energy felt like Lawndale; they felt like birthdays and Christmas; they were attached to memories, to Great Grandpa, Grandpa, Grandma, and Uncle Oka. They were touchstones to some things I could never have again, where great grandfathers die of old age, and grandmothers die of emphysema. Moreso, these were the things that carried those memories, or energies of those memories, these many talismans of what a trip to the mental and emotional gallows in only two years would be to come.

Fortunately, those two years had not yet passed but would come.

For this reason, a tragedy on a scale of immeasurable childhood proportions, that our house—the house that hated my family—*woke up.*

The root cellar was a deep place beneath the house, and fitting to its description, a sharp(ish) incline down a dirt path into the heart (and *stomach*) of the house on West Grand, where the house—and it was a house— sat on a foundation of stones and cinder blocks at its perimeter, and wooden stilts beneath its sturdy (if not unreasonably creaky) floorboards, and carpeted rooms.

I often remember the door to the root cellar being a little different than the door to a medieval dungeon, heavy and wooden, latticed in wrought iron and with as many rivets holding it together. To an eight-year-old, it may as well have been. The reality was not too far off from this, though. It was a door constructed of multiple four-by-eight wooden slabs, about three and a half feet wide and just slightly shorter than the average door.

That sharp descent of a dug-out path into the belly of the house required that adults duck a little entering the root cellar, and as in so many cliché tales of terror, what light was eventually installed there hung from a single wire in its bowels, from the rafters above, casting shadows in every direction, every which way.

One day, for no reason and without explanation, Mom talked with us after we got home from school.

Unless there is an adult, no one is allowed in the root cellar anymore.

It was not an open negotiation. It was a declarative and final rule.

STORMY

Between the setting and hasty exposition, I've been so busy fumbling through memory that I forgot perhaps one of the most important people in this story, which is saying a lot because he wasn't a person at all; I forgot Stormy.

It is 1986, late in the afternoon in Lawndale, after school. He introduces himself to our family under a thick blanket of black clouded skies. Those angry clouds that cover infinitely in all directions choke out the sun.

In this perpetual dusk of inclement weather, Mom ushers my sister and me out of the house into the yard.

Dad is home, smiling as the sky rumbles in a thunderous complaint about the dryness of autumn in Lawndale and a promise that rain is coming. It is a memorable moment here in Lawndale, Dad standing with the gate open under what I anticipate being a beautiful storm approaching.

The sky is dark, and I am filled with excitement and anticipation. *Yeah!* Dad is home from work. My sister and I were always happy when Dad got home, but this isn't why I'm filled with excitement. There is something else. Dad leaves his place at the fence and opens the back passenger door of his car, and there, seemingly out of nowhere, this blur of shiny black fur, floppy ears, and wagging tail rushes past him into the yard, making repeated laps around its perimeter as Dad shuts the gate behind him. The doggy speeds around the yard, his tongue flapping along the slide of his cheek like a windsock.

No one's talking. Dad's smiling—grinning, really—and the doggy charges us headlong. Mom is well... Mom. The doggy continues his charge toward us, and just as he arrives, Mom thinks he's going to bite, to attack. She lashes out inelegantly with a closed fist and grazes the dog's snout. He yelps, and immediately, instantly, she's sorry she did.

He forgives Mom without a second thought, jumping and licking.

In his body wagging excitement, he knocks my sister over. She's crying, and our new doggy, well, he's very concerned. Dad makes a sharp noise at him, a stern *hey* that catches the doggy's attention, but he was already sorry before that. My sister is crying because it startled her. Doggy is pushing his head against her, licking her, and pawing his apologies.

Mom is relieved. *Oh, he's sorry.* She consoles my sister, who is then a four-year-old with grubby, grabby little kid hands, petting the black Labrador affectionately.

He didn't mean to do it and made sure she knew. It was an accident. He's a good boy. He swears it. He'll be good for the family.

Memory is faulty in people, and there are holes in this memory that I can't patch. Missing parts between the lightspeed rush of a full-body-tail-wagging black Labrador and the only minutes that pass until we are gathered around him, huddled so that he is the center of attention, his head turning between all of us like a cartoon that can't make up its mind on who it wants to look at. He's a smiling, floppy black Labrador. Dad asks me what I would like to name him.

I don't know, and I say as much.

When the remnants of my family reminisce on this part of the story, there isn't a matter of contention. Sure, some details we remember differently, but well into the future, those of us still here will all agree that Mom is the first to suggest a name, and it is the dumbest name anyone could ever have suggested for a dog.

Extra points to Mom for knowing the toys and cartoons I love, though, as good mothers should.

How about we name him… Megatron?

Oh, Mom. Transformers? Really?

I am now in the presence of my family and its newest member, the most incredulous six-year-old that ever lived.

No, that's dumb.

Looking back on this, I must laugh now that I have my kids. Children at that age are so blunt and direct, without remorse. If I were a single man without children, this memory would still be funny, but it is more amusing because I am a father with three of my own. As a woolly-headed kid, I would never have guessed what tragedies the future would bear down on my luxurious head of thick curly hair.

Being a time-to-time victim of this sort of commentary myself, from my experience in having kids of my own that comment on my non-existent hairline (...but Dad, you have no hair), it is incredibly hilarious. I get it. I understand.

Yet, this isn't the present. This moment is still thirty-six years prior, and in the presence of my family, for a time, I would never have imagined a forty-two-year-old version of myself documenting this story.

At this moment, I am happy. This is *mine*.

I'm six, in the company of my family, and a big wagging puppy. I'm staring into the clouds again, and down the street they're as thick a blanket as they are in all the infinite sky I see above me. It's beginning to spit—maybe even sprinkle—and thunder rumbles through the inky, angry clouds overhead. I'm disappointed because I know that lightning makes thunder in a storm, and though I could hear the rumble, I couldn't see the flash, but I had a name for our dog.

Thunder, Lightning, and Storm Oka.

Mom's face is an expression of skepticism that mirrors my incredulity only moments before. Dad's face isn't much different, but he has a solution.

How about we call him Stormy for short?

He's the all-star, the family M.V.P. now. He's all our best friend, and I can attest at this moment what I cannot know while in 1986 but can tell you in the present, this wagging, floppy, clumsy puppy named Stormy is the only hero in this story, the only member of the family that can do what he would do in the years to come.

Stormy. *Such a good boy.*

And that brings us back to 1988 and *the lies we tell ourselves*.

THE LIES WE TELL OURSELVES

Dogs age quickly, and while Mom meant what she said about the root cellar, an eight-year-old and a six-year-old could justify that a two-year-old dog was, at the very least, a teenager, and that was close enough.

I mentioned that there are points of contention between my family and me, what we remember and how, but I swear and attest to it again: What I'm going to tell you *is* what happened.

It was a school day, or rather post-school. My sister and I took the bus home. It dropped us off at the bus stop on Merrill and Railroad, which, if you had to guess, was a street near a railroad. Makes sense. We walked home, and while I do not remember why, I knew that Mom had to go out for only a moment, but Dad would be home very shortly.

Mom says, to date, that she never ever left us home alone, and for the most part, I can state that is true. Whatever she had to do, for all I know, it was in the neighborhood or a quick run to pick up cigarettes. No idea.

The most important part of this point in the story is we were told: *stay inside, don't answer the door,* and *your dad will be home.*

Well, my sister and I didn't. The safest dog in the world was our dog, Stormy. Protector of the household, protector of our family, but especially protector of my sister and me, in no uncertain terms. We exited the kitchen entrance into the backyard, played with Stormy in the yard, and neglected to pull down any of our orange tree's impressive yield.

We avoided the farthest part of the yard, by the fence line, by the pomegranate shrub, just in case we had to get back into the house before Dad got home or before Mom came back. To be clear, it would make little difference either way.

Looking back, I recognize whether we were by the kitchen entrance itself or in the yard, there was no way—no matter how fast our legs could carry us—that we could get back into the house undetected if someone came home, mainly because there were two ways in. It was fine. After all, there couldn't possibly be any danger, not with Stormy on the lookout.

After a while, though, the backyard became dull, and so began our quest to the root cellar.

Mom said not to go down there without an adult. Still, Stormy, we reasoned, being a seasoned home and family protection veteran and being figuratively older than we were, was good enough as anyone. If something went wrong, Stormy could handle it. What could possibly go wrong?

The root cellar's heavy wooden door was shut, held closed by a single bolt latch. Mom or Dad could have locked it. A master lock, a padlock. Zip ties. A sandwich bag twist tie would have been better than nothing. It had been a place that drew our curiosity since we moved into the house on West Grand. The moment it became a place forbidden from exploration without the company of an adult, its allure was impossible to resist.

Down we ascended into the darkness, my sister and me.

The descent sometimes forced us into a trot that could lead to a jog, which could lead to falling, but thankfully, that never happened. With Stormy's company, I fumbled with the light switch until the single hanging bulb burned out the darkness, casting long shadows in every direction.

I remember dust motes swirling from the fine powdery dirt floor of the root cellar, kicked up by Stormy, my sister, and me. Stormy stood around, looking bored but happy to be in the company of my sister and me, his tail wagging intermittently in his lazy fashion.

Old bicycles, not *our* bikes, were stored on a rugged dirt ledge just between the stone and cinder block foundation along the edges of the house; older ten-speed models were caked in dirt and left forgotten by the previous tenants. A sparse network of thin, interconnected copper pipes ran just slightly above the rafters below the kitchen, the hallway, and the restroom; older plumbing, still newer than the original pipes, but God help you if someone turned on a cold tap or flushed the toilet while you were showering.

There was an unintentional theme in the root cellar, that hole beneath the house on West Grand. Everything was brown. The dirt ledges and walls, the underside of the floorboards and the rafters, the stilts on which the house stood, and even the boxes in our storage, boxes that we never unpacked; those old dust-caked bicycles on the hard dirt ledges. It smelled of wood and dust, but neither damp nor musty, and though the dust motes swirled in the air around us under that stark light that cast such long shadows, the air below was not unpleasant, though I can still taste the taste of the dust in my mouth.

We found the boxes—our boxes—and handled old toys haphazardly, my sister and I, discovering newer and newer old toys that somehow, we missed during our last expedition, things we thought were lost entirely to us, somehow restored.

Our bedrooms weren't small rooms, neither were they large, but it was a certainty that there was no room to unpack our boxes fully. This retreat into our nostalgic reprieve was the only place and way we could connect with lost time. We didn't even play with the toys so much as hold them for moments before placing them back in exchange for another.

I can't remember if it was one of us, or both of us, who first noticed the change in the atmosphere of that old root cellar, that hole beneath the house; I can't remember what caught my attention or what activated that sudden sensation of indescribable dread. I can recall that Stormy began whining, and then he laid down and curled around my feet, looking frantically back to the entrance.

In the cinematic experience—in movies—in these situations, the characters shiver or breathe out a mouth of frosty breath as the room grows cold. The light flickers or burns out, swinging on its cord, hanging from the rafters as the last bastion of light in the darkness.

If that were the case, it would have been better. At least that was something tangible to see, hear, and experience, but no, for us, it was only the terrible silence that accompanied the building dread.

No, regretfully, the temperature didn't drop until patterns of frost formed on surfaces or the fog of our breath became visible before us. The light did not swing on its cord, flicker, or burn out. For my sister and I in the root cellar, there with our brave dog and our unpacked boxes, there was an unequivocal nothing. For all the lack of cold, frost, or foggy breath, the blood in my veins felt as though filled with cold itself, and I felt the sensation of falling, that roller-coaster feeling; that feeling I know now is fear.

That feeling fed itself in perpetuity.

Then, without warning, the worst thing that could have happened did.

From where we were below, we heard something above us, *something* in the house, something heavy enough to creak the unnecessarily creaky floorboards above, and it instilled that deep dread: that sensation of free falling into darkness without knowing where it stopped or what waited at the end of that drop.

We all know that feeling at some point in our lives, some of us more often than others. Stormy was visibly upset, and I beckoned him, patting the top of my legs just above my knees.

Dad was home!

That had to be it. We must have missed it. He must've pulled in and parked, and we didn't hear it. Perhaps he passed the root cellar without us seeing his silhouette as he did; maybe he trekked the concrete steps, those four steps up that elevated porch to the kitchen; perhaps he went inside quietly, stealthily, shutting the door behind him without so much as a sound.

People mostly only lie to escape punishment. Most people hear the word punishment and think of some literal, even physical, consequence because of that punishment. Still, so many interpretations fit *far* too comfortably into the word itself.

My sister and I had told our share of whoppers in our youth, but habitually lying wasn't a common practice. In those days, until now, I suppose—and for everyone in general, I think—when something is wrong, something inexplicable, something frightening; when something distinctly off is in progress, I will lie to myself, and I believe that maybe everybody does.

Remembering my limbs shaking with fear-induced adrenaline, the loose dirt floor of the root cellar powdery and soft under my shoes, I understand distinctly now what I did not understand back then.

There is a theory whose results are inconclusive, though I tend to lean toward its affirmation more than not, as I have experienced it firsthand at that moment. If you have never heard of *gaze instinct*, it's simple. As humans and omnivores, we are predators and prey creatures in the food chain. While we may no longer sleep in caves or by the bonfire, guarding our tribes against some prehistoric saber-toothed predator, while we may have advanced technologically, our instincts did not get that memo.

> **Gaze Instinct (noun):** the feeling you are being watched; the knowledge you are being observed.

In the root cellar that afternoon with our good boy Stormy, my sister and I didn't know what a gaze instinct was. I can't even be sure if my sister sensed it, too, or if her growing apprehension was building around mine and even Stormy's, but I sensed it—*felt it*—and every part of my gut instinct making red-phone emergency calls to my brain via the vagus nerve.

I didn't know back then that my stomach had as many neurons in its lining as in a cat's head. I didn't think I could pick up subtle—even micro—changes in my environment. I didn't know that even though I couldn't see that we were being *hunted*, my amygdala knew it.

My survival instincts had been ignored, so my body pushed me to understand that something was going on; something was wrong. There were predators in the brush—bestial eyes on me, my sister, and stormy.

What I was feeling was fear, and not from some imagined place. It was a *genuine fear*, and as I forced myself to slow down and find a way out, something next happened that still echoes in my head.

There were heavy, deliberate footsteps in the kitchen on that sturdy, sometimes too creaky floor above us on stilts over the house's foundation on West Grand, our house at that time (but *not* our home, *never* ours). Heavy footsteps, but the kitchen door neither opened nor closed. How stealthy Dad must be. You could hear from the root cellar if the front door or the kitchen entrance opened or shut.

Obey the lie, Oka. Believe the lie.

Let the lie be true so that the worst thing that could happen is getting yelled at or a spanking. I wished this to be true because, even though I didn't know, *I knew*. I understood it wasn't Dad.

Those deliberate, heavy footsteps from the sturdy, creaking kitchen floor, slow and intentional, continued into the living room, the hallway, and the restroom. I half expected to hear the toilet flush—which, in some almost funny way, would have been a degree of relief.

From the kitchen, through the living room, into the hall, then into the bathroom, and then *nothing*.

I kept telling myself we must have somehow missed Dad. I clung hard to that lie as my mind spun its proverbial cogs and wheels, even as another lie began to develop, the lie I would have to tell my dad when I went into the house to find him there, asking why my sister and I were in the root cellar. My mind began to weave another lie so I could avoid the belt end of corporal punishment for my willful disobedience, mainly because the root cellar was somehow dangerous enough that we could not go down there without an adult.

Amid formulating lies, I realized it *was* a dangerous place to be without an adult, and not because of any storage that could topple over, fall on, or crush my sister or me. Back then, I couldn't put the knowledge into words; I couldn't understand what I was beginning to comprehend. That's not how a child's mind works.

I didn't know who felt it first, whether it was Mom or Dad, but something new was forming in my still yet not fully developed brain, something I wouldn't fully understand until my adult life.

Humans, omnivorous creatures that we are, are predators and prey in the food chain. Young animals aren't nearly as wary as they should be in nature. There's a reason that predators pick off the young animals in a herd. They're less awake, less aware, and less cautious of their world as they graze and roam. Parents protect their young; the herd forms around them. They kept the predators away as best they could, and Mom tried to do that.

I didn't know that then. My sister and I were much more aware of danger than any other young creature. We understood there was such a thing as danger, and we were mindful of apparent hazards such as stray dogs, steep ledges, and flying a kite during an electrical storm, but real danger? You hear about strangers and kidnappers, you hear about feral animals, and generally about the horrors of the world, but you never think it can or will happen to you. Interestingly, we are so averse to dangerous people while living in a constant state of it. That we can function at all is a miracle. From the moment we wake up until we go to bed, we are constantly threatened by danger in the world around us.

Our survival instincts allow us to blur our focus on the ever-present dangers of the world around us so that it can function while still reminding us through amygdalin vigilance that risk is still there, even if we cannot see it or consciously perceive it.

Children are especially susceptible. My sister and I were no exception, and Stormy seemed right on top of it.

I didn't use profanity in those days, but I can promise you the word shit sped through my head in repetition as I grabbed my sister's hand and hurried out of the root cellar, now ready to tell nearly formed lies if I had to. To save my hide, the lie that Stormy had gotten into the root cellar and my sister and I went to fetch him.

Even as I resigned myself to the fact that I would willfully lie to a parent, Dad, Mom, or both, I can still remember my hope of getting caught red-handed. Even as it developed in my head, I knew there was no way anyone would ever believe that story. I knew it was a trash lie, and I knew no way anyone could or would believe it. It was not logical to imagine that despite the root cellar's slide latch bolt being latched in place, poor good boy Stormy could somehow disengage that latch, pull it back, and scamper into it.

My sister and I hurried back up to the entrance, and I remember Stormy brushing past us, running out of the root cellar like his dog life depended on it. We shut that root cellar door and bolted it shut. We hurried up the four large concrete stairs and through the kitchen door.

You've seen the clichés, the horror movies. *You know.* You never call out into the unknown. I knew that, and I was only eight, but the lie I needed to tell myself *had* to be the truth for me more than any lie I intended for my Dad, Mom, or whoever was home.

Hello?

There was no one in the house, but I knew that. Worse than calling out into emptiness was the silence that called back. Our house, from the dining room table in the kitchen, the couches and coffee table in our living room, to the neolithic desktop computer in our den; from the hall and its passage to our three different rooms, no one. *Nothing.*

Outside, no cars were parked in the front, on the side, or by the garage.

No one was home but my sister and me.

There, while exploring the remnants of a once unbroken childhood beneath the house, in what I knew after that to be its belly, but also the place where it slept, while my sister and I ignored Mom's warning and broke Mom's rules, the house on West Grand *woke up.*

My sister and I grew up in the company of a whole family. Mom and Dad were all we ever knew through the first part of our childhood, and we suffered when that went away. When Mom and Dad decided to try again, to pick up the pieces of our broken family and put them back together, we clung to that. We found it in memory, and we found memory in the things we had from back before this all began. That's what we found in our old toys, but after the footsteps in what we knew was an empty house, we stopped going into the root cellar without an adult.

Or with one. Or, to my memory, again, for the remainder of the time, we would live in the house on West Grand.

My sister never told Mom and Dad we went into the root cellar, and neither did I. I was an honest enough boy most of the time, and if I did something wrong, I usually told Mom and Dad immediately because I felt guilty otherwise. I didn't tell Mom and Dad about the root cellar. I didn't tell them about the footsteps in the empty house. I didn't tell them the house had woken up. I made a new lie I only told myself. I wove together the story that anything I thought I heard was merely the house settling.

After all, the house was resting on that stone foundation, cinder blocks, and stilts behind that dungeon door that led into the hungry belly below the house on West Grand.

CHANGES

Things were changing. There was a new tension in the air, and it wasn't just familial or marital issues. Since that house had woken up, opening its wide maw to inhale us, I had concluded it hated us, as I suspected it hated those who lived inside its walls before us.

The footsteps had not been enough. The house and the things in it, whatever those terrible things were, was about to debut.

It's Wednesday, October 26, 1988. Parkridge Elementary School is at capacity, and the classrooms are a barely manageable mess. I was the new third-grade kid, and the day had not gone particularly well. No one in my class was a friend. My friends went to other schools or were in different classes than me.

Kids know, without knowing when someone else is different. On top of being the new kid in school but still a year away from a tearful conversation with my mother about ADHD, I was that kid—the one who was hyperactive and couldn't pay attention in class unless it was a subject of interest to me. That was costly. My classmates had three views of me: some politely tolerated me and almost treated me as their colleague; some snickered and laughed at me behind my back and to my face; and others bullied me.

Kids are cruel creatures and not remotely as self-aware as some people would try to have one believe. They act without consideration for consequence, just as my sister and I did when we descended into the dangers of the root cellar, not understanding that Danger had more faces than those found in the physical world. Kids may understand the concept of consequence but don't employ forethought when acting. They don't consider what they say or do or how it may affect others. They see someone different from the herd, and as animals in nature, they reject it, exclude it, and push it out.

Fortunately for me, this day was easily one of the better, maybe one of the best. The usual bullies, Steven, Javier, Danny, and Jorge, left me alone. Irene and Marcella, two of the class's designated mean girls, did not snicker, laugh, or make fun of me. Understand, I say bully, and I mean bully. Still, as a troubled child who attended a school where I was regularly bullied, as a third grader, I had unintentionally made an example out of three sixth-grade students who, during a morning recess before school, thought they were going to fight me and beat me up.

That was not the case. Instead, at the fight's conclusion, there were three hurt, bruised-up boys from a couple of our school's sixth-grade classes. Further, one of them now had a missing patch of hair where I had torn some out while trying to prevent him from getting away from me.

I don't remember the fight. I can only recall the beginning, when they approached me, and the end, when one of the recess ladies pulled me back from the three crying sixth graders laying in the dirt.

This led to some serious shit. Parents were called, and sixth graders were suspended. But I need you to understand I, a grief-stricken and broken boy, did not want to hurt anyone at this stage of my life. For all the mean girls and bullies, for all the burden and weight I carried, everyone was *always* immediately forgiven by me.

I wept the day I was forced to defend myself, not because I'd gotten hurt or because I feared getting into trouble—which I did not—but because I had no memory of what I did to the poor boys who'd played the role of predators thinking they'd found a weak and injured creature.

I can't account for the darkness of the modern age, but there was a time when you could stick up for yourself, and no one would touch you again—even if you lost. Which back then, I never did.

That single fight earned me enough reputation that, in the future, my bullies chose their weapons in words, mental, and emotional attacks, but never violence again.

The next day began well enough. Blanca passed me a note while Mrs. Napolitano taught a math lesson on the whiteboard.

I should tell you that the whiteboard was a new technology for our school and this time. Only a short while earlier, it had been a chalkboard.

I opened the note, and my heart fluttered *so* hard. I smile occasionally when this memory surfaces because I remember how it felt. The classroom was situated with desks for two, side-by-side, and I was assigned the seat next to her. She'd caught me looking at her several times, not often, but to steal a glimpse. Sometimes not briefly enough, and sometimes because she was stealing glances of her own: she, the pretty girl, and I, the gangly long-necked giraffe of a boy.

I remember staring at the note, butterflies filling up my stomach. I remember my cheeks felt hot, and I felt like the entire class was staring at me (though they were not). I remember her pretending to work on her assignment, aware I was gaping at the note, and quite aware that I knew she wasn't working.

Do you like me? **Y** ☐ **M** ☐ **N** ☐

Funny thing.

The "M" was for "maybe." *Maybe* wasn't a standard option on these notes. Perhaps it was a polite opportunity from the young Blanca for both of us to save face or dodge rejection.

I firmly believe that teasing can and does develop thick skin and character. However, teasing was precisely something that made me an anxious child because my dad teased me too much. My fear of admitting feelings for a girl wasn't born out of a fear of rejection or being bullied in school. It was solely taken from what went on at home.

…it usually starts at home.

From time-to-time, we would spend time together at recess, walking around the playground, or sitting on the swings next to one another. We seldom said much to one another, and not just because there was a slight language barrier. I couldn't speak Spanish, but she could speak English well enough conversationally. Sometimes, she would make eye contact with me, and those few times, we would spend recess together, and it was strong enough that I could not maintain it.

I was the weird kid, the odd-man-out, the one the herd would cull if they had the ability (they did not). Being an ADHD kid, before anyone understood what ADHD was (in fact, this will come up in the story), made me a target often enough, but today—well, today was the silver lining—with young Miss Blanca waiting patiently as she pretended to review her worksheet.

If I marked an ⊠ on "Y," there would be temporary happiness between us until our elementary school crush burned out, as those things do.

It was nice of her to leave a safe option, the *Maybe* option. If I marked an ⊠ on "M," it would become a recess conversation that would turn into an exchange of "you first" and "no, you first," and one of us would eventually admit something.

Mom believed that teasing was a necessary rite of passage in childhood, at home, that it built character, thick skin, and the ability for someone—especially someone like me—to function in environments where I would be the butt end of a joke. To this end, she was correct.

While Mom knew when to stop, Dad would sometimes tease me until I was inconsolable and then get angry at me for showing frustration or anger for what he considered harmless. This was a matter of contention between my parents. Mom practiced temperance, and Dad could occasionally have a malicious edge.

Bad as it sounds, I should be clear that home life was not an around-the-clock minefield of being teased or tormented by my parents. It is especially relevant in the twenty-first century that I have observed a pronounced lack of almost an entire generation's ability to cope with being teased. The way I was raised, there was nothing anyone could say at school that would embarrass me, get under my skin, or get to me.

Sticks and stones. Rubber and glue. And whatever else we used to instruct our kids.

I was tried and tested, so no amount of schoolyard teasing would affect my decision to mark an ⊠ next to the "M" or even the "Y"—if I wanted to. I wanted to admit it, but the same social vaccinations I got at home that emboldened me to stand up to bullies and deflect any schoolyard teasing or jokes made at my expense also subdued any courage I had at that moment. Blanca was still patiently waiting, and I had to decide.

I marked an ⊠ on "N," weighing out what would happen when I got home if somehow it got out to Mom and Dad that a girl and I at school liked one another. My sister attended the same school as me, and at her age, she would either hold it over my head or tell my parents. I couldn't have Mom or Dad knowing that. Ever.

I passed the note back to Blanca, and already, there was growing regret in my heart. Children feel these kinds of things are hard, which is now silly to me. I remember and reflect on these things with fondness, even passing up on the chance to have a girlfriend. There was someone in my class who—in what is admittedly one of the most challenging periods of my life—wanted to hold my hand or look at me. Or just be in my company. That was such a rare thing in my academic social life.

She read the note, nodded, and returned to her worksheet, except that she wasn't pretending to work on it anymore. She did not speak to me again after that, not that she was ever rude or unkind. She addressed me with the same polite disregard as all the others who weren't making fun of or bullying me.

By the end of the semester, the seating arrangements were changed anyway.

It wasn't some silly missed connection over an innocent childhood crush that frustrated me. Anxious kids with ADHD and some degree of social ineptitude are easily their own worst enemies, far more so than anyone in their class or school could be. It was hard: how someone like me punished themselves, the opinion

I held, and how I hated myself for being different and unable to fix it. But it wouldn't matter by the next school year.

Traversing through the fog of memory, whose passages are scarred with not just the fear that I may lose my family but also genuine terror, is no easy task. You step into these murky waters with no idea what you'll turn up, what you'll unlock or remember as you delve deeper into something you didn't intend. I can smell the damp morning grass. I can feel the Santa Ana winds blowing full force against me on the playground. I can still see the gray brier carpet of the classroom and the whiteboard that stretched behind Mrs. Napolitano the entire room's width.

By the end of the school day, I forgot about my regret in making a decisive *No* to Blanca. The buses arrived shortly after, and I waited in a line of other kids (only one different from my class, Danny) and boarded Route Fifty-Seven to the Merrill and Railroad drop-off. The entire ride home, even Danny was friendly to me. This didn't excuse all the behavior until that moment, but it made the ride home pleasant.

My sister and I disembarked at the Merrill and Railroad drop-off and began our walk home. We cut through the alleys that crisscrossed between the houses in our neighborhood, passing the friendly dog (a boxer) chained to his doghouse on the way into the alley.

We arrived home just in time for Mom to greet us at the back porch steps, standing in the kitchen doorway entrance.

Mom worked the swing shift as a waitress. When Dad got home, Mom went to work. I can't tell you too much about what happened until later in the evening; I don't remember. Yet, come dusk, Dad would make dinner and, after dinner, help me with my homework. Later, after my sister went to bed, Dad would let me stay up late with him to watch television. This is a significant memory for me, one both cherished and dreaded.

Thirty-four years later, I still have nightmares.

1984. WEST LAWNDALE, CALIFORNIA.

We lived in a small house in Lawndale, a place that was just a short walk from the railroad tracks and a short drive from *Leo's Mexican Food* restaurant (it's still there). The Pacific Electric Redondo rail lines intersected our street, separating my neighborhood from the one immediately after the tracks.

Sometimes, when the train went by, Mom would take me out to watch it pass, and she'd always point out the caboose. 1984 was the last year trains would use the caboose.

Our neighborhood was quiet enough, and there was a specific scent in the air that was always present, a freshness I haven't smelled since (but I know if I dared to return, it would still be there). As an adult, I can only describe it as the smell of memory. I think most people who played outside as a child can say, in one way or another, that there is a smell they probably can't describe, except as the smell of memory, from their childhood neighborhood.

We weren't the golden age Americana type of family who knew, by name, every neighbor and their families. We were the family who said hello in passing, kept to ourselves, minded our business, and wanted others to do the same.

However, there was one neighbor who most of the neighborhood seemed to hold disfavor. He was older than my parents, heavyset, often in blue denim jeans and some old tank top shirt or an old tee shirt. He wore a blue ball cap over a head of curly hair slightly longer in the back, but not quite a mullet.

He was not a social neighbor, which was fine, and it wasn't a problem that he didn't even attempt to ingratiate himself with the neighborhood. The problem was his dog, that squat bulldog that snarled and barked at all hours, who would follow along his chain link fence line when anyone passed, raising his hackles, and baring his teeth.

I had to pass this fence to get to my friend Sammy's house (I had a friend in the neighborhood, and he lived at the house closest to the train tracks). It is irrelevant, but this neighbor, whom nobody seemed to like, would often leave his sliding gate open. His dog, uncollared and unleashed, would wander out of his yard.

One day, while walking home from my friend's house, that dog was out and wanted to get me. The safest place I could find to escape was in the back of an old blue pickup truck whose tailgate happened to be down. The dog could get his forepaws onto the lip of the tailgate, but it couldn't jump high enough to get in and do more than bark and snarl guttural growls. I stood in the back of that truck; afraid it would get in and get me. I yelled and screamed for help, but my front door was too far away, and Mom couldn't hear me. The neighbor, whom I can almost certainly presume was the truck's owner, wasn't coming outside.

The next thing I know, I'm scooped up in a woman's arm, and she has a hose running, full faucet, with the garden sprayer set to stream, and she's spraying the hell out of that mean dog. I don't remember much more than that. The fear of being hurt by that dog is what I remember most, and then the recognition that it was Sammy's mom who'd come to my rescue. If you were to look at Sammy's mom, she was a petite woman, but she had the instincts of a mountain lion when it came to children.

I'd thought no one had heard my screams for help, but Sammy's mom must have been watching me trek home, and now she had the dog in full retreat. The next thing I remember is that she handed me off to my mom. I was alright, but Mom was angry at the neighbor for reopening his gate.

That dog is going to hurt someone. That can't happen again!

Then I was home, calming down. Safe.

I still remember Sammy, but not his mom's name or voice. I'll never forget her face, though. She was such a kind woman; she saved me when there was no one else.

There is a lot of blurriness between the scenes in my early life, where the mundane has been filed away in deep memory storage, perhaps to revisit in fragmented dreams or surreal nightmares.

As far as the more unforgettable memories, this would lead to a chilly Autumn night when I was supposed to be asleep but instead was awake in my bed, watching black and white movies on UHF (all the regular channels had signed off, and the normal stations were replete with static snow).

Some of you reading this may have no idea what that is or have only heard stories about the era of tube televisions. The younger of you may not be aware that the first color television released to the public in 1953 was an RCA. Yet, they didn't become mainstream until the mid-1960s.

These details aren't so crucial to the story, save that I had a black and white television in my room that was as old as my parents. This small, heavy tube television— maybe a thirteen-inch screen—was encased in silver accented wood-print plastic and featured two knobs— one on top, one below it.

Each knob had a dial, and the primary dial was numbered two through thirteen and then UHF. UHF usually featured public access television on some channels, but other than PBS (sponsored by viewers like you and Sears Roebuck), most channels returned static, or what we called "snow" back then.

Until somewhere between 1994 and 1996, a decade or so later, television stations went "off the air." After the last show of the evening, the channel would play the American National Anthem, and after concluding that, the channel went straight into snow. No primary channels would be available until roughly around 5:30 AM, when that channel would go back on-air, beginning by replaying the American National Anthem.

This was when the world was supposed to be sleeping, a time when distraction didn't keep us awake, binge-watching episodes of our favorite shows. Back then, streaming didn't exist. AT&T had officially shattered the Bell telephone monopoly, and Mark Zuckerberg was only seven months old.

The world slept, programming went off the air, and unless you had a video cassette player (VHS or Betamax), your remaining entertainment might have included reading a book.

Despite this, there were some stations you could find on UHF that played old reruns of Godzilla movies or other foreign films dubbed in English, and this is what Mom and Dad usually left on for me in my room, because in the dark silence, my brain didn't turn off. It didn't stop. It didn't just let me go to sleep, and often enough, it still doesn't.

Background noise was the distraction I needed. The volume was low, so it was a steady but unintelligible, boring droning that would lull me into dreamland instead of keeping me engaged.

So it was on that night, in the Autumn or Winter of 1984, that I was not sleeping. There was some movie on, something Japanese with men in futuristic construction suits leaping high over some machine in the center of the room. It wasn't particularly interesting, but it wasn't uninteresting either.

What I know about commercial breaks on UHF channels in 1984 could not fill a thimble. However, I can confidently say that public broadcasting networks have fallen to other uses (usually municipal) since the June 12, 2009, FCC requirement for all televisions to switch to digital frequencies. Still, when the movie was cut to a break, it was time to change the channel and see if anything was on. The commercials were long, and I knew I could still check a couple of other channels. I got out of bed intending to change the channel but never made it to the television.

I don't remember what I was doing until that point where I was up well past bedtime, into the late hours of the night. I don't know what I had done earlier that day or the next day's events, but I remember this.

The memory comes to me in both sight and sensation. I'm out of bed (I shouldn't be) and on my way to change the channel. It's a comfortable temperature in my room, but a wave of cool radiates from my bedroom window. The street outside is empty, and the streetlights cast their pale white glow on the pavement. I don't know why or what caught my attention, but something out of the corner of my eye drew me to the window.

I pressed my face to the glass; my left cheek smashed up against the cold windowpanes. Down the street, there is *something*. It's green, but not alien invasion green.

The word for this color was one I didn't know then, but I know it now, and I'll tell you, it was phosphorescent.

It was a luminous phosphorescent green, emitting only the slightest glow, so much that it was clear what I was looking at. It didn't scare me, and something in me as I watched it reassured me that while it was there, it was not *really* there.

At the end of the street, just close enough I could make out some of its features, was what appeared to be a ghostly hobo. It was solid-looking, not translucent as people imagine ghosts to be.

He was too far away to make out his face, but I could see he was smiling. His arms were animated like he was conversing with someone else I could not see. It occurred to me that whoever he talked to was no more there than he was. Because even at the young age of four (going-on-five), I knew what I saw was just a memory or echo.

I remember this feeling, particularly interested in his conversation, fascinated with the apparition of a hobo not having a lively conversation with someone I couldn't see.

I can close my eyes and still feel the cold glass on my cheek, still see the phantom hobo in his loose-fitting jacket, arms moving with the conversation. I still saw him offering a drink to whomever he was talking to. This was the first time I remember seeing something I knew was not alive but whom I also knew could not hurt me and was not really there.

The echo of the green hobo continued for a short while before fading into the darkness of the street. By then, the English-dubbed Godzilla movie had returned to the screen, and I fell asleep shortly after that.

1984 is where my earliest concrete memories exist, most vital in the form of sounds and smells filled with nostalgia. The longing for these memories is something I could not recreate for myself. These feelings are interesting. I could go back to any of these places (whatever places still stand), and if I had the resources, attempt to relive these moments, and they would never feel the same.

I will later do something that is a writing taboo. Without spoiling it, I'll attempt to demonstrate a perspective that is solely why this work is a creative nonfiction piece and not just a focused autobiography. I will describe how someone perceives time and how time isn't a matter of seconds, hours, minutes, weeks, months, or years but rather a passage of feelings, darkness, and light.

I think for children and sometimes adults, this is much the same. As children, we live with such a short vision of life, from weekend-to-weekend, holiday-to-holiday, so that we can play with our friends and enjoy grandma's refined cooking. Christmas eve (at least in our family's traditions) was a favorite time when the entire clan came together to overcrowd a house and exchange gifts. Those are how we count the days in childhood,

Not Monday through Friday, but instead from school into school out.

As teens, life is a combination of Monday through Friday, so we can get to the weekend and focus on winter, spring, and summer vacation. It becomes a combination of counting the days until milestone birthdays and longing to be an adult. Time passes in an excruciating slow crawl, but also so quickly we scramble to steal it back (but we never can).

Then something terrible happens.

We stop counting in days and weeks, and life begins a countdown in *years*. We grow up, get jobs, pay rent or mortgages, and life becomes year-to-year until, eventually, it's counted in decades. We watch our children grow so fast that we're afraid to blink while they count weekends and holidays until they, too, experience the slow crawl of time that will begin to move far too fast for them to perceive it. One moment, we are one way, and in the next, Mom and Dad have gray hair, grandma and grandpa are gone, and we face a terrible stark reality.

Somewhere along the way, the very memories that shape us become the only thing we have of the people who were there to help build them. All of this applies to the bleak certainty that sure as these things were and are intended to be the natural course of our lives: we are born, we live, and we die. However, in 1984, these things were still the furthest thought from my mind.

I looked at Mom and Dad, and I only saw Mom and Dad. Their names (Erin and John, respectively) didn't exist, nor did the life experiences, memories, and life journeys they experienced before becoming parents.

They were just Mom and Dad, with that assigned sense of them being the safest people in the safest place in the world. They would keep me safe, protect me, and assure me that the horrors in this world were only in my imagination.

There was no such thing as a monster. There was no such thing as ghosts. Nothing was in the closet, under the bed, or lurking outside the bedroom window. The wind, the sounds of a house settling, and the subtle flickers of shadow and movement were because I was tired. These are the lies they told us, which we perpetuate, not from a place of malice but because we want our children to feel safe. We lie because we want our children to be wrong because we are scared too.

It sounds terrible when you say it out loud, but what are the alternatives? You don't tell a child that there are evil things in this world beyond explanation. You may warn them about evil men in white, windowless vans and describe them as monsters, but ghosts? *Other things?*

So, when a child screams out in fear at night, a parent must first reassure them there is *nothing* there. Nine out of ten times, that's probably true for most people.

It was just not so for us. Not for my family.

OCTOBER 26, 1988:
THE WOMAN BEHIND THE DOOR

Mom had a rule: no scary movies or shows before bed. *Michael has an overactive imagination, John. He can't see those kinds of things before bed.*

I can remember the sound of her voice, and I love the sound as much now as I did then. Mom knew, you see. She knew my mind could take me to dark places within the recesses of my imagination and unresolved anguishes: the troubled child of parental separations, reunions, and whatever other things in the back of my conscious and subconscious mind that haunted me. She knew many things troubling me, though not precisely what they were or how often.

Nevertheless, Dad and I watched *Unsolved Mysteries* episode 1.3, which included the *Legend of the Tallman House*, the *General Wayne Inn,* and the *Haunting of the Queen Mary*. During its original run, this episode only aired on television twice.

Why would I know something like that?

This episode had a fundamental effect on me. If you're my age, you know this episode or probably do. You've seen it. Maybe it scared you, too, because it was from an era in which none of us were truly desensitized to fear. Even now, I can watch any horror movie or scary ghost story without a rise in my pulse.

However, this episode will affect me for the rest of my life. Not because I consider it a scary episode to this day, but because the memory smells like my dad's Brut cologne and sounds like my father's commentary, especially on the *Haunting of the Queen Mary*.

It was a wrench. It sounded like a wrench. It sounded like someone was banging a wrench.

That's the key. The wrench is somehow the key to that story.

What, Dad?

Nothing. She just kept saying the word wrench a lot.

I imagine my dad's inner dialogue made its way out, and he hadn't intended to discuss it aloud.

Why had it been such a compulsion to explore that hungry place below the house, enough that the house woke up not too much earlier in the month? It had, to some degree, in its way, demonstrated that it could make noise that didn't come naturally, and as I said, tonight, it would make its debut and demonstrate itself and its capability in living color.

This episode of *Unsolved Mysteries* scared the hell out of me, and I won't tell it any other way. In fact, when I discussed it with my friends, they described it the same way I did.

In 1988, television didn't have a content rating system. The only time you really might hear something like, "...what you are about to see may be disturbing to some audiences." was when the news was showing something no one wanted to see, except for the morbid curiosity an audience could not resist or deny.

Television wouldn't have a content rating system until around 1996—and even then, it would be voluntary until 1997, when the FCC put it into effect for all broadcasting stations that aired television shows.

Unsolved Mysteries episode 1.3 did not have a content warning, and I imagine it was because people who were supposed to know children of a certain age probably should not be watching. To date, the content rating system makes about as much of a difference to people in television programming as it does in video games and music, which is to say very little difference.

We watched (through commercials and all) the entirety of the sixty-minute episode, and afterward, it was late for both of us. Dad, who got up every morning at 4:30 AM, showered, shaved, and slapped on his Brut cologne, and then he was usually in bed by 8:30 PM, which, consequently, at eight years old, I was expected to go to bed as well.

It was roughly 9:45 PM.

Bedtime, a tuck-in. Then, Dad went to bed.

The house was silent, but not the peaceful silence that rocks you off to sleep. These days, I was consciously afraid of my room—scared of something I couldn't see and didn't entirely understand, and though I knew something was wrong, I didn't know what.

It is established that my brain is always running on overdrive. By the time of our triumphant family reunion from its fractured separation only the month prior, Mom and Dad had given me an old analog alarm clock radio, the kind with the needle and dial and the little thin brown wire that hung out its backside as an antenna.

As always, Mom and Dad tried to find something dull, so I wouldn't be engaged. I never particularly liked sports as they were boring, so Dad set the dial to an AM sports radio station.

Even back then, that station came in so clearly for such an antiquated piece of technology.

At least it came in so clearly until it didn't.

The rule at bedtime was that the door could stay open, but only halfway. After Dad tucked me in, he shuffled to his room to sleep. I lay there in bed, listening to terrible baseball audio reruns, trying to clear my head and my heart of the fear I was feeling. Some of it was from the episode of *Unsolved Mysteries*, but I was fearful that night, especially that night.

I thought of the root cellar and the heavy footsteps, calling out *hello* to no one and having the terrible silence of nobody calling back in return.

That terrible silence was the same now.

Static on my radio, being that it was so clear and so in tune with its station, was unheard of until now. The static wasn't just an ill reception but *something else.*

I heard the static; then the station changed, but not to static.

I heard static, station, static, different station, static, *different station.*

The needle on the radio was moving; I didn't see it happening, didn't see it moving, but I knew it was, and in the aftermath of what would come, there would be a horrific vindication in such a suspicion.

The stations were changing and passing back and forth. I knew better than to look at anything. I'd seen scary movies and learned to keep my eyes on anything other than darkness or open space, so I leaned out of bed, placing my palm on my carpeted floor. I reached for the knob on the radio with my free hand. I put that damned needle back where it belonged, but as soon as I released the large flat knob on the side, it started moving again.

Blood was like ice in my veins; my stomach dropped like a roller coaster, and something moved.

The door, maybe not; maybe only subtly, almost indistinguishable, except the hungry bestial thing was *there.*

It was there, and I could tell in the same way prey animals know when predators lurk nearby. I saw the silhouette behind my door.

I started lying to myself. *You know that feeling, too, don't you?*

I called out to the shape as though it were my sister hiding in the dark space behind my door, that half-open door whose hall light only spilled to the foot of my bed, that half-closed door whose shadow between its interior and the wall was far too dark, far darker than it should be, I called out. So, I lied.

I'm going to tell Dad. Stop it! Stop being stupid.

I said that often (*Stop it!*) because I knew that wasn't my sister. I knew it in my heart, gut, and soul as gooseflesh crawled over my body beneath my Batman-themed pajamas. The thing behind my door *was not* my sister.

My room suddenly smelled foul; a stench I'd never known was suddenly in the air. It smelled like rotting meat and old garbage, the smell of decay—the dead smell of a dead thing. Even though I knew, I was still unable to understand what I didn't know. I knew if there were such a thing as ghosts—and having seen what I believed to be by memory to some degree, my small share of these such things—that they, apparitions, did not do this (the green hobo was there, but he wasn't there).

There are no afterlife experts, master paranormal researchers, scholars, scientists, or investigators. It's a lie people are desperate for an answer to accept because it makes the unknown feel known.

No experts exist because expertise requires research, study, and repeatable results. For that to work, whatever they are, well, they would have to cooperate or do the same thing at the same time (or maybe not even at the same time) repeatedly to demonstrate their presence.

No experts. Especially not me, not then, and no matter what I thought I knew in that moment or of that experience with ghosts, I didn't know any more than anyone else. So, I lied again.

Stop it! You're being stupid! I'm going to tell Dad on you right now!

I can still hear my voice in my mind, that poor kid. The dwindling bravery, me rolling back onto my bed, propped up on my elbow, no longer the courage or constitution to risk having any part of my body on or near the floor.

It moved, and I knew then it wasn't like the phosphorus hobo by the railroad tracks. No, this was different, something else, this thing, this manifestation that held a silhouette behind my door, this presence that was changing the radio station. It stared at the floor; I knew it wasn't a movie. It wasn't the kind that can't or wouldn't hurt you.

And it knew that I knew it was there.

I couldn't tell you how or why I understood that. The lie I created that this was somehow my sister (who was sleeping peacefully in her room) was long dissolved. You see, it moved its arms, hands beneath a tattered, heavy-looking fabric, staring at the floor, and just when I thought it couldn't get any worse, it did.

It stopped whatever it was doing and slowly looked up from the floor, locking its stare on mine.

A badly decomposed (or decomposing) woman has two pitch-black, hollow, and empty sockets where her eyes should have been. I say her, but I mean it.

It stared at me, and I stared back, and for a moment, I couldn't muster a sound—not a scream, not a cry for help. It was there, a solid-looking apparition, not the translucent monsters from some movie, but something physically present in its appearance, and I will never forget that face. There were no words. There are no words, but there was a scream, and mine was high and shrill as I shrieked out.

Dad's bedroom door opened down the hall to the right, and he was in my room before my scream died out, the light on, the corner empty.

The woman behind the door! I bawled like the child I was.

The woman behind the door. The woman behind the door. The woman behind the door.

I don't know anything about ghosts. No one does. Not truly. The things we see when tuning into our favorite (or less than favorite) paranormal entertainment or paranormal reality television programs, the stuff we read in books, the things we see in movies; all of it is based on conjecture drummed up during the spiritualism movement that first gained traction in the United States in the mid-1800s.

There are no canonical texts on spiritualism, no scriptures on how or why these things happen. *Because* there is no definitive evidence beyond anecdotal evidence, there is nothing verifiable. In the early days of the US American spiritualism movement, people drew on old wives' tales, word of mouth, and oral traditions. Sometimes, they created dogma to fill in answers where there were none.

What are ghosts? Are they earthbound spirits who failed to, refused to, or did not know to *crossover*? Who decided that spirits *crossover* or are somehow *earthbound*? There are no written instruction manuals like the one in Tim Burton's *Beetlejuice*—no *Handbook for the Recently Deceased* advising that "...functional parameters vary from manifestation to manifestation."

The remnant embers of the spiritualism movement, as well as the paranormal enthusiast community (hobbyists, ghost hunters, paranormal researchers, paranormal investigators, psychic-mediums, etc.), cannot even agree on what these things are or are not. Anyone who says they are a paranormal expert lies— even if they don't know it.

No one knows. With exception to legends, traditions, and theories (from which almost all the current information on hauntings is based), there has never been, and may never be, proof of whatever these entities are.

I believe one thing. If there are ghosts, they sure as hell don't look like rotting corpses or incomprehensible horrors. We spend so much time applying the rules of life and its natural order to the study of the paranormal, leaning on pseudoscience like it's a foundation when, in fact, it is a crutch.

That moment changed me forever.

Since then, in a lifetime of nightmares, its rotting body creaks with old grinding bones. Its neck cracks, dry vertebrae beneath decayed cadaverous flesh as dry as old jerky, and staring up at me with those unseeing holes where eyes should have been.

You can cope with that and pray, but it doesn't go away.

I live well over five hundred miles from Corona, California, and that thing is long behind me, but here it is, taking up rent-free residence in my mind. Mom said my mind goes to dark places, my imagination detailed in 8K high definition, and I can smell it right now in my memory, see it, and hear the sounds it didn't make because imagination takes personal horror and makes it far worse. *This happened.*

Hello, the house said in the broken silence of my shrill screaming. *Hello, here I am. See me.*

My sister heard me screaming that night. I couldn't imagine *anyone* could sleep through that, though she never left her room. She asked questions, innocent interrogatives from the mouth of a six-year-old little girl. *What was happening?*

Mom and Dad reassured her that I'd only had a nightmare, but I wasn't convinced Mom and Dad believed that. At the time, I was oblivious that they, too, were experiencing a creeping fear as hungry walls in a hungry house chipped away at their armored responses to its actions.

October ended without further incident, a thankfully anti-climactic conclusion to our *first* month in the house on West Grand Boulevard.

KIDS AND THEIR STORIES

Now, in the rear-view mirror, October saw us in a blissfully uneventful but short-lived period of peace.

I was not to bring up the Woman Behind the Door. Mom and Dad impressed upon me the importance of that, that it had only been a dream, and there was no point in telling my sister. Mom and Dad insisted it would scare her.

November would mark the start of our second month in that house. Though October had come and gone, I felt like a year had already passed. Time is different when you're a child, and what passes so quickly as an adult drags by when you're only eight.

Life returned to relative normalcy. Mom and Dad weren't fighting much, and the tension seemed to disperse. We went about our lives in a typical fashion, waking up and going to school, coming home, and doing whatever homework and chores had to be done. Depending on the day of the week, my mom or Dad would cook dinner, and my sister and I would watch cartoons and go to bed.

Though October was over, as it was for a period of every generation, the topic of the popular urban legend Bloody Mary reared its head. I quickly learned the origin story of Bloody Mary was a topic of contention, and nobody seemed to agree on who the legend of Bloody Mary was based.

The first candidate is purported to be Mary I of England, daughter of Henry VIII and Catherine of Aragon. Why? Mary I of England allegedly burned over three hundred religious dissenters at the stake.

The second candidate, a notorious favorite among school children, is Elizabeth Bathory, who allegedly killed over six hundred fifty girls and women to bathe (yes, literally *bathe*) in their blood.

The last candidate is Mary Worth of Lake County, Illinois. Mary Worth is as much a legend as she is a real person. She intentionally interrupted Harriet Tubman's underground railroad, offering escaped slaves false quarters and then shipping them back for a bounty. Her legend continues that she may have been invested in the dark arts and may have practiced these arts on an indeterminate number of the enslaved people she deceived.

Ultimately, the legend ends with a lynch mob on her property, where she is captured and burned at the stake, and then her remains are buried on her property.

A few of the claims on this last candidate for Bloody Mary came from a ninety-year-old Lake County resident in the 1960s, who claimed she was a young girl when Worth was burned at the stake.

Whoever Bloody Mary is, whichever of the candidates—*if any*—and however the urban legend began, one matter is agreed upon: summoning Bloody Mary requires practice in catoptromancy, the mystic practice of divination using a mirror.

However, I should clarify that Bloody Mary's legend requires no catoptromancy expertise. The most complicated versions require a girl to walk backward upstairs with a lit candle and chant Bloody Mary's name in the mirror a specific number of times. In this version of the legend, Bloody Mary presents either the face of the man you will marry, or the visage of a skull, suggesting you die before marriage. That may be the *most* benign version of the legend.

After that, it gets very dark. In other versions, Mary appears, haunts you, drives you mad, or kills you.

My sister wasn't willing to play this game, but it was a topic of conversation in school. For my little sister (at six years old), it went from being a topic at school to an issue at home, with my Mom and Dad doing their best to dispel any ideas that had any truth to it.

This was why I couldn't ever discuss the woman behind the door.

It was a pleasant Sunday. My sister and I played outside, played with friends, played with Stormy, and enjoyed dinner with our family. We settled into the living room for a movie and watched *Harry and the Hendersons*. It was time for us to go to bed after the movie.

After our usual bedtime routine, we all settled into bed. However, with Mom and Dad home, we had two parents tucking us in, closing closet doors, and checking under the beds. Nothing could go wrong with two of them tucking us in. *Right?*

The day's playing had worn us out. For the first time in a long time, I slipped peacefully into a sweet, dreamless sleep, and this time, there were no ghosts to wake me, no woman behind the door. There was no dread. I was a happy kid asleep in record time without sports radio to lull off.

My sister didn't have such a fortunate night.

THE BLOODY MARY

I woke up to the adrenaline rush, flailing beneath the tightly tucked covers, the sound of muffled screaming called through my bedroom walls. I was covered in cold sweat, even though it was relatively warm in my room. My eyes were locked on the space behind my door, but there was no one and nothing there.

I heard running and saw Mom and Dad's silhouettes rushing past my half-open door, throwing my sister's door open as she bellowed for help. I was already out of bed and in my sister's room, which I didn't want to be. Mom was cradling my inconsolable sister in her arms.

This, I'd never seen before.

My little sister sobbed, choking on her tears, gasping between breaths. Everything was happening too fast, and everything was so sharp. The room was too bright, the corners too quick, and the expression on Dad's face was something well beyond concern. Even as Mom hushed and soothed, she stared at my Dad.

My sister wept, but she said something that sent a current of cold through my veins, and my breath escaped me.

Bloody Mary! My sister pointed to her wide-open closet door.

This was strange at the time—the closet door being open. You know the nightly routines of childhood. No one's closet doors were open, and neither I nor my sister would risk opening them after bed. Not for any reason.

Mom and Dad eventually calmed her down. Still shaken, she explained she was sleeping when the lights came on. She woke to a sharp noise, her closet door opening, and out of her closet, a terrible form crept onto its feet, staggering toward her.

The Bloody Mary, she said.

Like the woman behind the door, Mom and Dad insisted The Bloody Mary was a bad dream. How the closet door opened wasn't a topic they could explain away, so they didn't mention it.

After that, it was agreed that she and I would change rooms. My sister would take my room, and I would take hers. It did help me a lot. I slept better in her room, and for no reason, I wasn't worried that The Bloody Mary would be visiting my new room anytime soon. I couldn't tell you why.

Things quieted down. Mom and Dad were doing better again, and it looked like there was hope for our family.

November was another cold month. I don't ever remember frost on the windows in Brea or Lawndale. Our morning treks to the bus stop on Merrill and Railroad were chilly, so Mom would heat the car and wait with us at the bus stop so we could be warm.

There were very few other kids at our bus stop, most of whom arrived only moments before the bus did. Mornings, when Mom waited with us at the bus stop, were moments of Zen. We made idle chit-chat, listened to music, and relaxed a bit longer. When the bus arrived, we shipped off to school at Parkridge Elementary.

Classes weren't overcrowded yet, and while there were bullies, I was mostly left alone so long as our paths didn't cross. It's not ideal, but I made do with what I had to. I didn't have to worry about fighting; my reputation kept that kind of attention away, even though I was not the type of person who would throw the first punch. Never the aggressor, at Mom and Dad's insistence.

The taunting and the teasing were kept to a minimum in the classroom, but Danny, Steven, Jorge, and Javier would—when I could not avoid them—attempt to goad me into fighting, put me down, or come up with taunting nicknames.

I shrugged it off. Nothing anyone could say was par to the teasing Mom and Dad could dish out.

As a child, teasing at home was frustrating. It wasn't a constant, but when it did happen, it was enough to drive me to tears sometimes. As an adult, I don't know that I necessarily approve entirely, but it did prepare me. Not everyone was going to be friendly or pleasant to me. That would apply to the rest of my life. There are assholes in the world, and you can't go knocking all of them out because they said something I didn't like.

The year 1988 was nothing like the world as we know it now, and the way it was then (or at least in my little world) required a kind of constitution that is rarer in contemporary times. Many people now say things like, *yeah, but you shouldn't have* had *to put up with that. Things are different now.*

As a father of three, I can attest in no uncertain terms that nothing has changed except the way bullies function. The internet and social media have made a shield for faceless accusers to spread their pain, gossip, and threats without getting caught so easily. This isn't something I discovered on my own. The National Institutes of Health stated in a July 2022 article that in-person and online bullying has increased suicidal ideation in children and adolescents.[1]

There are programs in place, contingencies, and laws passed since 1988 to help prevent it, but children will be children and behave as children do without thinking of the consequences (their own or others).

So, as a third-grade kid recovering from a marital near miss between my parents and a sometimes-troubled

---

1   "Cyberbullying Linked with Suicidal Thoughts and Attempts in Young Adolescents." National Institutes of Health, July 21, 2022. https://www.nih.gov/news-events/nih-research-matters/cyberbullying-linked-suicidal-thoughts-attempts-young-adolescents.

home life, the cruelty of other children took a back seat as I tried to get through it all.

November happened quietly for our family. There were sensations of foreboding occasionally, and no one wanted to go into the root cellar unless they must. We slept with our doors open, and even Mom and Dad occasionally left their door a fist's length open. No one questioned why, and no one volunteered an explanation. We all understood that "bad dreams" could happen without warning, and open doors made it easier to get to one another.

Cold and quiet, the month passed quickly enough. But strange things continued to occur. There were phantom smells, like rotting oranges or a foul and inexplicable odor, and uneasy sensations, including the overwhelming feeling of being watched.

Just before bed, we heard someone screaming outside our front porch one night. Dad checked it out, but there was no one there. The following day, while my sister and I were playing on the front porch—atypical of anything we ever did—I found a full upper bridge of false teeth set in silver. I called Mom out, and she told me not to touch them. She picked them up with a plastic grocery bag, wrapped them up, and threw them away.

At this time, we weren't very concerned about crime in our neighborhood. We knew some of our neighbors more than others, but for the most part, ours was a safe neighborhood if you discount the presence of the malicious entity we lived with.

Just before Thanksgiving, my sister was playing on the front porch. The door was open to the house, and my mother was in the living room. I was in my room playing by myself. Suddenly, my sister is crying, and it's not fear; it's pain. Mom rushes outside to find she'd fallen into the red Bougainvillea bush next to the porch, though she's accusing me of pushing her into it. I hadn't, and Mom explained that I was in my room.

The Bougainvillea bushes are pretty and grew thick and tall. They also had near-inch-long thorns on their stalks and branches and were sharp—my poor sister.

The conversation went in circles. Mom continued to insist she fell. My sister relentlessly insisted she was pushed. Mom tells her no one was there to push her and brings her inside to tend to her scratches.

Mom later asked me if I had anything to do with it, and I told her I had nothing to do with it. Dad then asked me the same thing, and without doubling down or getting upset, I told him the exact truth I told Mom.

This scared them and they became angry, but not angry at me. They're angry and scared because there is something that can *touch* us and they are powerless to do anything about to stop it or to protect us from it.

DECEMBER 1988

Thanksgiving was fantastic.

We dined like royalty at Grandma and Grandpa Denney's new house (and what would be the final home they owned) in Fontana, California. The whole family was there: uncles, aunts, and cousins. These family celebrations were larger every few years as the young grew up and had families.

With Thanksgiving behind us, we entered December. It had gotten even colder since November—a cold I'd never experienced. The days were warm enough, and we—my sister and I —played outside. Some days, we played with Erica and Jessie, and some days, we played with Robert and Jessica.

School in December was a strange thing. The kids were kinder, which I attributed to the season's spirit.

Nights were getting easier, too, or at least so I thought. One Sunday, after no short amount of pleading, I convinced my mom to watch an episode of *The Simpsons* so she could see it wasn't whatever negative hype she'd heard about it. After that, it was smooth sailing. I even had the old thirteen-inch black and white television in my room again—that same television.

Secretly, I'd been watching *The Simpsons* since the *Tracey Ullman Show* back in Brea. At first, she, my sister, and I shared a room. I slept on the floor at the foot of the bed. Mom would come to bed after work and watch television. It was *The Tracey Ullman Show* with a *Simpsons* short (which I always watched), and usually, I'd fall asleep before or at the start of the show *Dark Shadows*.

On Sunday nights after dinner, I could watch *The Simpsons* in my room, and my sister would join me. Sometimes, she fell asleep on the floor, and when it was time for bed, Mom and Dad would cover her and leave her to sleep.

The house, for the most part, had gone back to sleep or was, at least, dozing. I had not seen, smelled, or heard any new phenomena for weeks, and I was growing comfortable and complacent in the new peace.

Excitement was in our household; Christmas was in the air. Family time was well spent among the four of us, and sometimes even Stormy got to join us. We even had a Warehouse Video membership card and rented movies for weekends. Our favorite was *Beetlejuice* (it was Dad's favorite), but it was one we could all watch again and again and enjoy. Other than the excitement of the Christmas season, life in our home had become delightfully dull.

The Christmas of 1988 was incredible. Christmas Eve began with Dad gathering my sister and me and returning to Gardena, California. We gathered at Grandpa Oka's house. We were the first there, and while Dad spent time with grandpa, my sister and I explored Grandpa Oka's backyard.

I remember he had a giant desert tortoise in his backyard when I was five. We would feed lettuce and play with it, watching it wander around the yard and do whatever tortoises did. He also had a chow he had gotten my grandmother back then. She named him Akai—the dog, not Grandpa Oka.

But that Christmas, it was a different kind of quiet there. There was no Grandma Oka or Great Grandpa Oka anymore. There was no Akai, and now, as I explored the backyard with my sister, there was no tortoise. Grandpa Oka said that one day, the tortoise burrowed into the ground to hibernate and never returned.

By the time we went back inside, my uncles were there. I remember this moment and thinking that things weren't the same.

They were all sitting in the dining room together— Dad, his brothers, and my Grandpa Oka at the table. There were no wives or grandmas. Neither of my uncles had kids of their own yet. It was sad for me.

When I was alone with my dad, I said it didn't feel the same, and he hugged and hushed me. He explained that he felt that way, too, and so did everyone else.

The Christmas tree at Grandpa Oka's looked the same as everything else, but it was the only thing that looked the same. We ate dinner, though I couldn't tell you what it was, opened gifts, and after a little more familial socializing, we left and went to Grandma and Grandpa Denney's house in San Bernardino.

Christmas there was enormous. Though there was a much smaller tree, there was a much larger family for balance. I played with my cousins and ran around the house. We played games on Nintendo in Grandpa Denney's room and went outside into the cold to play.

Dinner was an enormous ham, studded in cloves, garnished with ringlets of pineapple, and slathered in glaze. Candied yams were baked beneath a hard shell of marshmallow, mashed potatoes, and salad. Grandma's homemade fudge, ambrosia, pineapple upside-down cake, and Christmas fruitcake comprised the desserts. I ate *all* of them, even the fruitcake, which I disliked.

Afterward, we all exchanged gifts.

Grandma and Grandpa's gift was last: my very own Nintendo Entertainment System. I knew that as soon as I got home, I would put away that Atari and set it up. It was a beautiful night; everyone was smiling, and I had never felt more like a part of a family than I did right then and there. I knew this would be how things would be forever, and nothing would ever change that.

NOVEMBER 15, 2022: REFLECTION

I started writing this a few short days before my mother's sixty-eighth birthday, spurred by a conversation she and I had a week before. I reflected for a long time on how I would write this, as I had attempted to do so with no success twice before.

I believe in hauntings, and I don't think this one was some *earthbound spirit* or *lost soul* looking to cross over.' I have experienced just enough and *so few*. I believe these spirits are rarer than people think. Some, like the radiant hobo I watched from my window in 1984, are just memories imprinted as three-dimensional projections that remain and are activated by indeterminate triggers.

Paranormal experts call these occurrences *non-intelligent hauntings*, and while I disagree with so many things—almost everything—that paranormal experts classify, I do agree with this one, as I believe I've seen it with my own eyes. Everything else, I can't pretend to classify. Life isn't a comedy ghost movie with spirit catalogs and manuals, at least none of verified repute.

The entities in the house on West Grand hated us, or whatever you want to call them. They attacked each of us when we were alone as often as they could and fed on our fear.

Nothing about that house was good.

After Christmas of 1988, 1989 came bringing more change to our lives. My sister and I would no longer have to wait at the school bus stop. Mom and Dad put us in the YMCA, and it wasn't long before we made many friends. The YMCA shuttled us to and from school, and either Mom or Dad would pick us up from the Y after work.

At home, things were darker. I spent 1989 dodging that house's hatred at every turn. Doors would open, or someone would knock when no one was around, but I coped the same way the rest of the family managed, through self-deception.

Knock. Knock—*don't worry, it's the house settling.*
The door slowly creaks open—*that's just the wind.*

By 1989, I understood why adults justified inexplicable activities as natural occurrences. It's so easy to ignore the wind or a house settling. Even when you know it's not the wind. Even when you know the house has long since settled. You brush it off, and it's less frightening.

My newfound way of deflecting what was happening around me was outright denial. It makes me laugh because I would never suggest denial is an appropriate response to potential dangers, but it helped me through 1989 while living at West Grand.

WHAT MY SISTER SAID

I have another story to tell you. It's not mine. It's my sister's, but it belongs to the house. All these stories belong to the house, don't they? I wouldn't know this story if not for a text from my sister, an afterthought from a journal she kept in her fourth-grade class.

We were long out of the house when my sister was in fourth grade. Whatever I thought was scary was nothing to my sister's secrets. There's no date in this story, but all we need to know is that it happened when we were in the house. It occurred after she and I switched rooms in December 1988.

How many times did she fall asleep in my room to avoid going to sleep in hers?

There was so much going on, and while the future looked bright from my perspective, my sister was suffering. In our recent correspondence, it was like I was a small child again and scared. She and I were sitting next to one another on the back porch steps; she confided her story to me, a terrible secret, except I was here, in my home. Safe away from whatever dark secrets were told on those old concrete stairs. There were many.

My sister attempted to fall asleep in my room as often on a Sunday as possible. Unfortunately, this passage doesn't take place on a Sunday.

It was well past bedtime. She was awake and alone in her room. She doesn't know why she can't sleep or understand why she's so afraid.

No, the word she used wasn't *afraid*. She said, *terrified*.

She got out of bed in my old room, which made her a braver person than I, feet visible to whatever things may have lurked under her bed, sky lining herself to whatever things lurked in leathery flesh within the darkest corners of that room.

A child should never have to learn the things she employed as she departed her room, checking the window behind her to make sure no one was looking in, checking corners, pulling the door open wide into her room as the warm hallway light spilled into her room, somehow making distorted shadows darker, and longer.

She checked her corners, right and left, in the hallway. My door was half open, but I was asleep. She crept down the hall, passing the bathroom and living room. Mom and Dad's door was open a fist length from the jam and silent. Silent in the same way it was when

I once called out *hello*, and pure emptiness greeted me back. It greeted her, too.

Mom and Dad's room was a safe place, and it was the only room in the house where the closets and the space under the bed were not a place of abject horror. This was where she went to sleep when no one was the wiser. She would sneak out of her room, creep into Mom and dads, and crawl under their bed to sleep.

She would crawl under their bed to sleep. To escape her bedroom and whatever that was in there that watched her, whatever terrible hungry monsters lurked. She was always afraid. Despite what I went through, I can't imagine what she was going through.

So, my sister crept into their bedroom, Mom and Dad's, and before she made her way onto her belly to crawl under their bed, she saw that their bed was empty.

Mom and Dad are always supposed to be there, and their absence was as bad as, if not worse, than whatever was happening in or beneath the house. I cannot emphasize enough the bravery of a six-year-old girl who left the sanctuary of her bed covers, from the weighted dread of her room to the emptiness of a place where her parents should have been.

The sheets were skewed, the space where Mom and Dad should have been, and nothing. No one was there. My sister gathered her courage and plodded out of Mom and Dad's room, through the living room, and the kitchen. Her tiny feet sounded heavy on the kitchen floor, echoing hollow around her and into that space beneath it.

She unlocked the door to the back porch and stepped outside.

The porch's concrete sent cold shocks to her bare feet and calves. Everyone knows this feeling at one point or another in their lives. A child's pajamas are no shield from the icy air of early morning hours, but my sister pressed on.

Down the steps, across the yard to the garage. Dad used this garage as his workshop, where he listened to music and escaped from the house. My sister checked the garage, but it was dark. No one was there.

My six-year-old sister, out there alone in the dark, was probably safer than ever in the house, but she shivered with both dread and the ominous cold.

This wasn't what she was looking for. She turned and hurried back up those large concrete steps into the kitchen, shutting and locking the door behind her.

She returned to Mom and Dad's room, and to her sudden shock, they were sleeping peacefully there. Dad slept utterly still on his side of the bed, and Mom was curled in a ball on hers, snoring like a lumberjack. Feeling relieved, my sister quietly got onto her belly, crawled under the bed, and slept.

I had never known this, never knew my sister was so scared of her room—my old room—but I understand. The only thing worse than seeing the woman behind the door (aka the Bloody Mary) was *not* seeing them and knowing they were still, watching unseen, leering invisibly by the bedside or hidden in the shadows.

Every corner, every turn, and every wall of the house was a place of deception. They inhaled our pain and exhaled their hatred. The house was nothing more than wood and plaster, but the unseen things that dwelt there gave it life.

These spirits are beyond our comprehension of time. To this day, I don't know why they were there in that house. I only know what living there did to me, and only recently have I learned the full extent of what happened to the rest of my family.

My sister's testimony sat with me for an entire day, and I wrestled with how I'd share her part in it.

In those old days, I wasn't necessarily carefree, but I was close to it. Though, like the playful teasing I endured, my sister suffered the practical jokes my dad employed on multiple occasions.

Don't get me wrong. Even when I smell Brut cologne today, memories flood back, and I remember for a long time, my dad, for all his shortcomings, was one of the safest people in my life.

My dad, who I sometimes call by his name John, was a genuinely good man. He had, like me, ADHD, screwed up from a childhood mine could not contend with and had maybe the emotional capacity of a twelve-year-old.

So, when my sister explained that on a few occasions when John had to trek into the root cellar, he would have her go with him, I imagine he didn't care for being in the root cellar more than anyone else.

John brought my sister into the root cellar, gathered the needed tools, and raced my sister out of the root cellar. Little legs neither stride as far nor move as fast up the dirt ramp to the door. And that's when he'd do it: go out the door and shut it while she was still down there.

He would hold it shut briefly—long enough for her to beat on the door—before letting her back out into the sun. Trapping her in there for only a moment, but long enough to scare her.

Trust takes a long time to build between people. It is almost unconditional between children and parents, even when the parents do wrong—even when they don't deserve it. There is no excuse for what John did. However, Mercy is in too short order in the world now.

John loved his children. He never learned how to be a proper father until it was too late. He was a hell of a toy. There was never a moment where he was unwilling to play with us, whatever the game or idea. He was the theme park dad, the camping and circus dad. John never missed a beat, tucking us in or reading us stories in funny voices.

John spent his life living too hard and too fast, looking for lost things he could never reclaim, but it wasn't always darkness.

A PAGE OUT OF THE SPRING OF 1989

Mom was in the kitchen with her then-best friend, Sandra. Dad was at the table. Leading up to that moment, they were hanging out in the living room, and Dad had a hilarious idea for a practical joke. He liked jokes. The set up was simple. My sister and I were to hide under the counters, under the sink, and under the utensils drawer where we kept forks, spoons, and so on.

I was eager to be a part of this. My sister, daddy's girl, was simply happy to make him happy. Besides, this was a joke. It would be fun. Who didn't like jokes?

From under the counters, we heard Mom and Sandra come into the kitchen and sit at the kitchen table. Dad joined in the conversation while putting on a pot of coffee. We heard him sit at the table with no tone of inflection to suggest that he knew the funniest joke ever planned was about to unfold.

The coffee was done, and Mom was at the pot, pouring herself and Sandra a cup.

I pushed the drawer out from where I was, and the kitchen was quiet. Then, my mom took what I had to assume was a spoon. I pulled the drawer shut from underneath. Sandra was talking to my dad, and they were chit-chatting pleasantly, laughing to punctuate funny things, but Mom wasn't laughing. She was trying to pull the drawer open, and with all my nine-year-old strength, I was pulling against her. Then I opened the drawer, and she tried to push it shut but couldn't.

"John!" She cried out. "Something is wrong. The drawer's broken."

So, to make this an authentic experience, I opened and closed the drawer slowly and then quickly.

"John! Something's wrong with the drawer!"

Dad laughed it off like, *don't be crazy*, though he never said as much and was wise enough not to.

Even Sandra discounted it, and then the drawer was opening and closing under my power, slamming shut, opening hard, slamming shut, and Mom panicked.

How hilarious, I thought.

Finally, I was feeling too cramped, so I opened the cabinet door. From where I was, the door was wide and shielded me, so when it opened, my sister was also coming out simultaneously, and we were both smiling with an expression of *April Fools'*. However, it wasn't April, and as we saw Mom's pale face and Sandra's expression of fear, we slowly realized the joke wasn't funny.

Yet—and I love my mom for this—once she got over the initial shock, my mom still laughed it off, and it made my sister and I feel much better.

But Dad was in trouble.

...THE FALL OF SUMMER

Dad smiled when he saw me coming in from the backyard on a Saturday afternoon. He looked at me with an expression I will never, ever forget. He had so much love for his son.

Dad and I had a time-to-time ritual on paydays. Every payday, he would take me to Corona's premier toy store, *Toy City*, a store I'm sad to report hasn't been around since the late 1990s.

That Saturday, just like I did every payday, I piled into my dad's van, which was a familiar feeling. We drove and made idle chatter along the way, laughed, and smiled at me at stoplights.

Upon arrival at *Toy City*, Dad said I could pick out any toy. The month prior, I saw Warren Beatty starring as Dick Tracy on the *Dick Tracy Special* with my uncle (a Los

Angeles Police officer. He would retire as a Lieutenant Detective). So, I already knew what I wanted.

Dad took me into the store, thinking maybe I'd get a *He-Man* action figure or something, but I was browsing something completely different in an aisle across from the front counter.

There, hanging fully stocked on the racks, was every character from the *Dick Tracy* movie. I shuffled through them and saw what I wanted. In a bright yellow plastic fedora, there was a striking likeness to the actor and character (or, so I thought at the time)!

I picked up the chosen toy and browsed through the rest of the aisles. The new *He-Man* toys were trash, as expected; the new cartoon was trash. Classic *He-Man* was way better—both the cartoons and the toys.

Dad asked me if I was sure that was all I wanted, and I insisted.

Dad paid for the toy at the counter using a cashier's check, which the cashier denied. Then, he attempted to pay with a money order, which the girl at the counter said *Toy City* didn't accept. My dad argued the point a little because they were *as good as cash*, but the cashier said it was the store's policy.

Finally, he used his debit card and paid for my toy.

On the way home, I thought he might be annoyed with the girl at the counter, so I told him it was stupid she wouldn't accept the cashier's check or the money order. Dad smiled and said she was just doing her job.

We cruised a little longer in a comfortable silence and finally pulled into the driveway. Dad and I exited his van and went into the back yard. I closed the gate behind me as Dad ascended the stairs and went in through the kitchen entrance. I sat on those concrete stairs and opened my *Dick Tracy* toy. I put his billy club in one hand and his gun in the other. I sat on the backyard porch for a while, playing with my new toy.

I'd wanted to get a bad guy, too, but I'd feel greedy if I'd asked for two toys. I was trying to be a good kid. Good kids keep stress off their parents. Stress-free parents stayed together.

I remember being so happy playing on the stairs and making my toy fight imaginary enemies around him. I recall Mom opening the door and asking if I could come inside momentarily. I shuffled up the rest of the steps, went inside happily with my new toy, and sat at the table with Mom, Dad, and my sister.

The happiest days of my life were spent together with my whole family. We watched movies, played games, and we did family things. The family was everything.

Family is still everything.

Birthdays and anniversaries, picnics, parks, and theme parks; it's all time well spent—spent well with the people you love the most.

Up until that moment, that had been a perfect day.

"Your father and I aren't working out."

Those words echoed through me for years to follow.

"It isn't anything you or your sister did, and we still love you both very much. We just can't be together."

My instinct was to let loose the tears and bawl. I felt nauseous. Tears welled up and spilled over.

"I knew it," I said. *Oh, not again. Not again.*

My mind scrambled as I remembered years earlier when Dad had left, and Mom held onto me as I cried. Then, later, after missing a visitation day when I was six, I had to excuse myself from a friend's house multiple times to go home and cry in my pillow.

Everything was ruined now. Everything was destroyed. Suddenly, I was just so tired.

The house was no longer my biggest fear. My biggest fear was there was no way to save my family.

Unfortunately, sometimes, we can't evade our fears.

The following years were comprised of court, counselors, and custody hearings. Judgment followed, and then visitation. But this time, I did not cry. Instead, I became angry.

I was angry at Mom but grateful she was the good guy in this ugly thing. Dad was also angry, but unlike me, he was more willing to express it.

I had seen my dad plenty angry before. I'd heard him and my mother argue in ways that would shame animals on wilderness shows.

Dad wasn't a bad visit, though I was angry. I was so furious at him because, in the end, Dad failed us. I know it takes two, but objectively speaking, Mom tried. She tried for years, and all that trying put us in Brea. She kept trying, and it brought us an all-or-nothing last chance to Corona.

As though the pain of twice losing my family wasn't enough, Mom moved us into a small apartment, and Dad stayed in the house on West Grand.

THE THINGS MOM
KEPT FROM US

I was somewhere in my mid-twenties when Mom sat down with me. We were catching up over lunch while eating our meal and sipping over soft drinks.

"Do you remember the joke you, your sister, and your dad played on me?"

I knew the one she was talking about; she didn't have to elaborate. I said I remembered.

"Did you ever wonder why that joke scared me so much?"

This conversation came up out of the blue. She relayed to me the incident in the kitchen with my sister and me joking on behalf of our father.

Did I know why that scared her so much?

No, of course not.

Mom looked at me like a professor looking at a student eager to learn something new. There were so many things we'd missed out on, my sister and I, and I don't mean happy family or missed moments. We missed the stuff about the house—things that happened to Mom, to Dad, things that scared *them*.

The "bad dreams" my sister and I had with *the woman behind the door* or *the bloody Mary*. Those stories had much less doubt than Mom and Dad led us to believe. In hushed whispers behind closed doors, they argued in sharp tones whether lurking things were beyond their perception.

Something inside them believed us, even when they eagerly told both themselves and us nothing was happening.

Mom had a bad feeling and ignored it. Much like all the adults who experienced Grandma and Grandpa Denny's house in Redondo, Mom ignored all the activity there.

Bad dreams. The house is settling. It must be the wind.

That house was long settled—the house was from 1916. But the house's walls were filled with misery, sorrow, hateful tragedies, and whatever else lurked beyond the scope of sight. The house wasn't settling when the horizontal blinds shook slightly behind the entertainment center.

Mom ignored it.

They shook a little more, with intention and purpose.

She called bullshit.

Mom had her favorite curse words. She had them for every occasion. She was surprisingly well-reserved with cursing around children. It's not to say it didn't happen, just on fewer occasions. However, at that time, Mom called out into the room's silence.

Bullshit, prove it.

A challenge if ever there was. But that time, the house answered back.

From the top of the horizontal blinds, maybe six feet up from the floor to the base of the windowsill, as though a single finger pressed down the horizontal blinds and dragged them down, one at a time, in rapid succession. They shook rapidly before my Mom could react, and the window rattled violently behind her.

Mom panicked and went to retrieve Dad, who wasn't gone yet. He always would come at a moment's notice; he was the hero of the household. However, leading up to the divorce, Dad and his Brut cologne came less often.

The lights were on throughout the house beside mine and my sister's room. The lights were on, and Dad calmed Mom. When she finally went to bed, at least she had Dad there. Initially, I said nothing was the only thing worse than an answer. That was not true for my mom.

So, that's how it went for Mom. It was the defining moment where suspending disbelief was no longer an option. After that, skepticism was an ally of hers no more.

Mom was wary of the windows in the kitchen. Practically speaking, she was afraid that anyone could break into the house through those six windows. Logically, she knew that outside, it was twelve feet from the windows to the sidewalk below the porch. The closest window to the porch was still six feet up and diagonal to the top step. No one was climbing through those windows, and Dad said as much when she voiced her concerns.

Yet, she still didn't find practicality and logic comforting. From the inside, those windows were still relatively high up. Once upon a time, they could open, riding tracks supported by small pulleys and a length of rope.

Those days have long since passed, though Mom wanted them fixed so she could open them on hot days and bring a breeze through the house. The longer she lived in the house on West Grand, the more disturbing and irrational the fears those windows instilled in her.

Irrational fears are those phobias that come all at once without explanation but can and are caused in daily life by environmental, experiential, and even genetic factors.

Feelings lie, which is a certainty—except when they don't.

Navigating life and learning when to trust your feelings versus when to subdue them is one of life's most significant challenges, though, by modern standards and studies, there may be something to gut instinct. There are as many neurons lining the human stomach as in a cat's brain, and that bad feeling—that gut instinct—*it knows*.

Even contemporary courses in personal safety and security now teach that, to some reasonable degree, human beings should trust their intuition. Article after article, from security professionals to psychologists and even scientists, tells us to entrust our gut (within reason).

No one felt safe in that house, and it wasn't just because of Dad's spiral into personal misery. Dad's personal, internalized feelings of inadequacy and inferiority turned into raw anger, and yeah, that anger was scary, but it wasn't constant.

That falling feeling, sometimes we love it, yeah?

Scary movies and rollercoasters. First loves and auditions. A similar feeling occurs when you're in danger. Like when you see the mountain lion a moment before it emerges from the brush. It's the same sense of danger in all living creatures.

That was the falling feeling we had in that house. It wasn't just the windows in the kitchen, the space behind our doors, or our closets; it wasn't just how the walls emanated a tangible sense of cold, hostile fury. When we moved to Corona on October 1, 1988, it was as though a subtle weight immediately dropped onto our shoulders, and it only increased when we set foot in our new house. As we settled in, we grew unsettled.

A lot goes on in our lives, and sometimes, we experience something we are not consciously observing but are picking up subliminally or unconsciously. Our built-in survival and warning systems blare red flags and sirens to warn us.

For Mom, this came from those empty, staring windows high enough to reduce the likelihood of home invasion to negligible odds. High enough, the sensation of being watched through them (or by them) struck the chord of the uncanny valley. They were individual empty spaces that, by daylight or by night, always carried an ominous aura of threat; these old and oblong rectangular things whose glass pooled thickest at the bottom, whose impurities visibly flecked our field of vision.

They bore the constant impression that something unseen outside was looking in or that the windows themselves were like watching *eyes* set high into the wall of our kitchen. It didn't help that she could always hear something tapping on the glass or the windows shifting in their sills as though something was trying to open them.

Were these events isolated, it would be fine, possibly disregarded as the wind or bugs fly against the glass. If you tried, anything could be explained away, but this happened too often, those windows shifting in their sills, shaking as though they were willing to lift on their own if not for the swivel latch locks holding them in place.

They weren't just stories or fables; the monsters were always there.

They were persistent, those malicious things on the other side of sight; those presences in the house on West Grand couldn't be explained away or imagined as some mundane things such as a settling house, especially when the phantom smells came.

Mom often smelled the odor of rotting citrus in the house. Corona, California, was well known for its citrus exports; more widely, Riverside county was primarily known for its citrus. It would not be unusual for the smell of oranges in the morning air or wafting in on the evening breeze. We even had an orange tree in our yard that produced an abundance of large, delicious oranges.

Still, the scent persisted for Mom, just as from time to time, the smell of death rose in the air around me when I was alone in my room or the living room. Just a tiny whiff here and there, sometimes lingering a moment.

Mom laughed when she explained that she smelled rotting oranges, making my dad look everywhere for rotting orange peels. She caught its odor often enough and asked my dad so frequently to find its source that it became a common frustration for him.

I couldn't tell you whether anyone else caught those phantom scents back then, but there was a lot I couldn't tell you about. I had no idea what was happening with my sister, Mom, or Dad back then. Maybe we should have discussed these things. Maybe communication could have seen us into a new house, somewhere else that didn't have a sinister presence lurking.

But we didn't talk about these things. No one said a thing, as though pretending there wasn't a problem was enough to make it disappear. That went double for my parents and their issues.

That's not entirely true. No, they weren't talking about things, but they sure as hell yelled about it— screamed about it, fought about it.

They did everything but work things out.

I think Mom tried, but my dad couldn't understand the idea of change. His childhood, time in the Navy and twenties were long gone. The parties and partying were long gone; while Mom grew up, Dad didn't want to. He desired to work in foreign lands and see the world—to take half-year contracts in Europe and experience the world as he did when he was young.

He wanted to do this while his wife and children awaited his return. Dad enjoyed a lot of things that a family made impossible. He wanted something back that he couldn't have, and that built resentment within him. He looked at us like a reef in rocky shallows and saw himself as a ship run aground on that reef.

Mom holds him accountable but maybe shows more mercy than I did.

Dad was twenty-four when I was born. When you're a kid, and your mom tells you that your dad was just a kid when his first child was born, you can't understand.

A ten-year-old sees a person in their twenties as so much older, so that concept is lost. I can say the same about how I saw him in my teens. I can even say that in my twenties, any time my mom told me Dad was just a kid when my sister and I were born, I couldn't understand. By my mid-twenties, I felt like an adult. I thought I did adult things, pausing to party with my friends or staying out until dawn.

I am a man in my forties now. I look back to my twenties and see someone I barely recognize. I see a good kid who was still a selfish teenager in his heart and head.

The echoes that the house left in me were still fresh, never far from memory, my heart, or my head. Always lurking, but then, whatever scars Dad left in me kept pace with the nightmares of that house.

The things Mom kept from us, my sister and I, protected us for quite a while. As children of divorce, we already had enough on our plates to deal with, and I know there are plenty of broken homes and children, and my story shouldn't be any worse than anyone else's. Anyone who has ever known a broken home knows what I mean.

As it was for John, life can't go backward for anyone. There's no undoing what is done. You're not rebuilding your past even when you pick up the pieces. You're using the parts to build a new foundation.

My pieces held me precariously over a deep emptiness—sorrow I'd never come to terms with, built not unlike a foundation resting on cinder blocks and wooden beams. Mine was as good a youth as Mom could provide, giving my sister and me everything she could and anything we wanted. She worked harder than I've ever seen anyone work to ensure that birthdays had cakes and Nintendo Game Genies, Easter had baskets, and Christmas had a tree and gifts beneath it.

It's strange how it all came from the shattered pieces of our family's failure: the failure of our parents, who were supposed to, for better or worse, in sickness and in health, for richer or poorer until death did, they part. It's true. It takes two to make something work. There were moments when Mom asked Dad to try again, and Dad refused; there were moments when Dad asked to try again, and Mom refused.

1990 AND THE TIME
THAT FOLLOWED

No one knew back then what things would be in the years to come, but for everything that didn't work, it's miraculous the way everything worked out, and the end was still seven years ahead.

After they were apart, Mom moved us into a small two-bedroom apartment. We left the school we'd been with when Mom and Dad decided they would try again, and Mom enrolled us in a new one.

Dad didn't leave the house on West Grand. Not yet.

Something I must constantly remember, something I must remind myself as a parent, is that parents are just people.

It's so easy to hold grudges when someone is on a pedestal. I still associate a safe feeling with the scent of Dad's cologne. I'm reminded of him when I see that green plastic bottle on the shelf in a store aisle.

Dad intended to stay in the house on West Grand until the lease was fulfilled. Dad could afford it independently, but that would not be the case. Not with the lifestyle he wanted.

When my sister and I weren't around, he was a free man to live the rock and roll life he wanted. Band practice every day in his garage if he wanted to do that. He couldn't accept it, as good a musician as he was, that playing cover songs from music two decades prior wouldn't land him a job in the music industry.

So, got a roommate. Thankfully, Dad at least had the sense to find the right one.

Bri was an older woman. Older than Dad had been and a divorcee, and she had a son the same age as I was. Dad kept the room he and Mom had shared, and Bri took my old room (the one I had when my sister and I switched rooms), and her son, who was there every other week, took my sister's old room—the room where I once saw the woman behind the door.

In that room were my bunk bed and my old dresser. The bed was no longer situated across from the door but adjacent. The rest of the things belonged to Bri's son, Jimmy. The rest of my things were in storage—in the root cellar. I wasn't going down there again, no way.

Fortunately, Bri and Jimmy brought a Nintendo, so I wasn't entirely bored between movies, games, and my old friends in the neighborhood. Further still, anger and all, I loved my dad despite everything.

So, Bri's boy got my bed, and I had to sleep on blankets on the floor at my mom's. Further, I felt like a second-class citizen at my dad's house. As you may guess, I got angry. I got mad. Sometimes, I lashed out. And Dad lashed back.

Not physically. We were past spanking anymore. Honestly, I would've rather him take a belt to my hide. So, from time to time, we'd argue, we would shout, and we would scream. Then, he'd see who he was yelling at—not my mom—but me, and he'd drop his rage all at once and attempt to make up, and we would.

I would forgive him instantly. I didn't know it back then, but now? Now, I realize that's what my mom had gone through.

When Bri lived there, I had to sleep in the room (especially tough when Jimmy was at his dad's). My sister hardly had it better, sleeping on the couch in the living room.

Eventually, Bri moved out. There was no word on why she left, and I never asked. I didn't hate the woman but didn't miss her either.

My sister got her old room back—*the Bloody Mary room*. After that, I chose to go to the living room, refusing to continue sleeping there. That room didn't belong to me. It didn't belong to Jimmy. That room belonged to whatever horrible thing hid in the shadow of half-opened doors.

That thing was still there—not just there but everywhere. I can't tell you if it was one or many, though I still suspect the latter.

Life became this thing we did. A week at Mom's. A week at Dad's. Over and over again.

Dad would use our weekends to do something fun. Idyllwild is fishing in Big Bear Lake in an A-frame cabin—no worries when we can't get a bite. He found us a trout farm, and we brought them in, one after the next.

I owe my love of fishing to three people, and Dad was the first of them. Every time I go fishing, I remember Dad and me fishing off the Redondo pier. We never caught a thing, not once, and it was fine.

The good times were good, but the bad times were so bad.

I can't tell you when it happened in the year, but it was a Friday or a Saturday because I didn't have school the following day. I was lying on the living room floor and watching a movie with my dad and my sister, and the day must have been long because the next thing I knew, I was waking up in an empty house.

I was alone. I was about ten years old, and for someone who knew better, I was about to make the mother of all mistakes. My first mistake was not trying to go back to sleep. But I hadn't woken up because I'd had a good nap or was done sleeping. I'd woken to a flood of adrenaline, and for the second time in my life, I understood how loud silence screams when your house is doing the screaming.

I'd woken with a blanket pulled over me, a pillow under my head, and my face cold.

The television was off. The den's light was off. The only light was the one overhead, a soft-watt bulb that didn't give off much light.

My mind spun; obviously, I'd fallen asleep, and everyone went to bed.

That's not true.

It wasn't true, and that instinct within said as much. No one had gone to bed, but even though I knew as much, I went ahead and called into the empty house, calling for my dad first and then my sister.

When they didn't return my call, I slowly checked their rooms.

Hall light, on. Yet, no one was in their rooms. I hurried back through the living room, into the kitchen (avoiding eye contact with the windows high up on its furthest wall) and opened the back door. Stormy looked up at me from the porch and gave me a couple of tail wags.

I shut the door and locked it.

That silence.

I could explain it to you in analogies, metaphors, and parables for a hundred pages and still not communicate its weight or vastness. My voice didn't echo off the walls, in the hall, or within the rooms. I was a ten-year-old boy whose voice spoke into a vacuum. No matter what filled the house, the furniture, the games, the movies, it was indeed empty.

I was shaking, trying to be Dad's brave son, but where was he? Where was my sister? Why was I alone?

I sat on the sofa as long as possible, trying to hold it together, but the house didn't creak. There was nothing—not a single sound. I began crying, and I won't forget it. I started crying because in all that silence, in the back of my head, I felt something creep into my thoughts.

There you are.

I rushed to the kitchen, ran to the phone on the wall to the right, and dialed my mom. Seven digits in, and it rang. Mom answered the phone, and I completely lost my shit. I remember trying to speak between snotty sobs, choking on my saliva with my back turned to those watching windows. Finally, Mom got me to a place where there was enough calm that I could talk.

I told her I was alone, that my sister and Dad were missing, and how scared I was.

God bless my mother. She lied those sweet lies, telling me I was safe, that there was nothing to be afraid of, and that my sister and Dad had probably just gone out for a moment. I was on the phone for five minutes when the house's front door opened.

This was unprecedented. We rarely used the front door, but there they were: my dad and sister with bags of fast food in hand. Dad saw me, and to his credit, he rushed to me. His face was bewildered. He didn't know why I was crying on the phone or the reason for my panic.

I was just relieved. The house was loud again in the way that sound bounced off the walls, and our voices filled it again with a life that hadn't been only moments before.

Mom wanted to talk to Dad.

Oh, no. What had I done?

I was filled with anxiety; I worried it was going to turn into another fight. Dad and I would yell at one another; my sister would hide in her room and cry. I'd spoiled the entire evening.

But Dad's face didn't look angry. He looked scared and ashamed. That conversation lasted five minutes before he gently put the phone back in its place.

The first words out of his mouth were a question. "Why did you call your mom?"

There wasn't anger or judgment in his voice, though he looked like a child whom an angry adult had admonished.

I didn't answer at first, mostly because I was still scared and relieved. So, he asked a second time, and his voice had a bit of an edge that time. So, I lost it again and explained everything about my fear and how I hated the house. I even said he knew why, smart enough not to mention what lurking evil hid in my sister's bedroom.

Dad wasn't surprised, which scared me a little more, but then he did something that I thought wasn't like him and, to this day, was out of character for the man at that time. Dad lied to me the same way Mom did. He apologized for leaving me alone and explained that he thought I'd been so tired he ought not to wake me. He and my sister decided to get some fast food and surprised me.

Usually, when Dad was wrong, he got mad at you for his being wrong. Then he yelled at you about it, the prideful man he was, apologized afterward, and admitted his wrongdoing. Mom had to have said something to him. I don't know what, but it shut him down, and he was a profoundly penitent man.

My sister and I slept on the living room floor that night. Dad slept on the couch. He kept the television on, volume low, all night, and to my great satisfaction, I slept uninterrupted.

DARLENE

As it goes in broken families, there was Mom, and then there was Dad. The differences between my parents were night and day. Mom tried briefly to date but never found someone worth her time.

Dad didn't have as big an issue finding a girlfriend. He was a funny, charismatic, fun, and good-looking man. Women saw substance and charm in him; even with cheap cologne, his allure was undeniable.

So, perhaps a little too soon, Darlene appeared. Bri was long gone, and Darlene was twenty-something to Dad's thirty years, and in her eyes, the sun rose and set in him. Two kids and a dog in a three-bedroom house with a job that paid well were hallmarks of the ideal man to Darlene, and Dad's life experience and his work as an aircraft engineer for a prominent aerospace company iced the cake. But could a man like my dad commit?

Darlene figured he had been previously married, so that must mean my dad could and would commit. She didn't question how she'd gotten into this relationship as soon as she did or why she was meeting his kids that early on.

I can't prove anything, and though from time to time, I talk to Darlene, who is old and sick, if I ever asked anything about when and how she met Dad, she would deny it, but I believe that Darlene was in my father's life before the divorce. Within days of my sister and I meeting her, she slept over. I've been twenty-something and moved in too soon with girlfriends in the past, but Dad had a chick habit. When Mom explained that to me, she clarified that there used to be a way some people thought when they knew their spouses were getting some strange on the side.

The first was not to ask. The second was the knowledge that a man might go out with his friends, drink at the bars, and meet someone for a quick fling in some sordid place, but at the end of the night, that man comes home to them. Dad always returned home to Mom. She knew, in theory, but she never asked, and he never told. There were no lipstick stains on the collar, no women's perfume on his clothes.

When I say Mom tried harder than Dad, it's not because I'm biased. For all the trials and tribulations, Mom was a mom first and has always been.

Darlene was friendly but stupid. She was a living example of youth being wasted on the young. She hadn't the wisdom of years Mom and Dad shared. She was pleasant but ignorant and sometimes jealous of my dad's attention to my sister and me.

Still, my sister and I liked Darlene at first. One evening, though, while we were all watching a movie in the living room, my sister asked Dad to sit beside her. Darlene chimed in, using a girly voice I'd never heard her use.

"No, sit next to me."

I could have forgiven that, but the fact that my dad went and sat next to her instead of my sister made Darlene the enemy. Like I said. She was a kind lady, but she lacked common sense, and sometimes, she was stupid.

A couple of weeks later, Dad did something stupid himself.

I'd brought up the house and finally dared to tell Dad why I hated sitting in the kitchen in the evening doing homework and how I could feel those windows staring down at me, or something just outside them, staring through them, down at me. I told him about the woman behind the door again. I relayed—reminded—him of the Bloody Mary, and I didn't care that my sister was there.

My list of grievances was long: the footsteps I heard in the root cellar, the emptiness of that house when I was left alone.

I remember that Dad had been thoughtful about it for a long time before he took a deep breath. If you have children or ever intend to, and your family comes to you about horrors in your home, move. Gather up the family and move. Barring that, please do not let your first go-to be trying to relate to them on the matter—especially not children.

"Darlene saw a ghost."

I remember how quiet it was. I finally asked Dad what she saw, my stomach dropping, that falling feeling, afraid it would be some monstrous creature behind their door or skulking out of their closet. Dad said he didn't know, but she would be over after work.

That day was otherwise typical, as my sister and I went out to play with the kids in our neighborhood. One certainty was that our friends remained for all the inconstant things in our lives. They were almost always home, and there was always a way to while away the hours playing in their yards or houses. It was an escape, however temporary, but worthwhile all the same.

When it was time to come in for dinner, Darlene was there. She sat in the seat my mom once did, and as Dad served us dinner, she ate at our table. I remember thinking that she was going to be around for a while. After dinner, as we settled into the living room for some family time plus ghosts, Darlene, I asked her if she actually saw a ghost.

Darlene insisted she had and led me to my father's room (what she called her and our father's room), and she pointed to her side of the bed.

Her side. The side my mom used to sleep on.

She said that earlier in the week, she had come home, and as she entered the room, a young woman was sitting on the side of the bed. She said the woman was young and beautiful and did not acknowledge her arrival.

She was there, and then she was not.

When I asked if she was transparent like ghosts in the movies, Darlene explained that she was not—that this ghost looked like a physical person sitting on the bedside and that, at first, she was just dumbfounded to see someone sitting there. Then, the woman was gone just like that.

To Darlene, like to me and my sister, these apparitions weren't movie ghosts. They looked like they were there, physically. Darlene's experience reminded me of my experience when I'd been four and had seen the spirit of the phosphorescent hobo.

The thing is, I was a ten-year-old trying to make sense of something that neither logic nor reason could be applied to. I was a kid playing junior ghost detective to discover why things in my life happened the way they did.

I couldn't control my parents' failed marriage. I couldn't stop them from divorcing. I couldn't prevent Dad from seeing Darlene. But if I could unravel the house's mystery on West Grand, then maybe there would be some answers I could cling to.

I walked through my life feeling empty, going through the motions, constantly fearing that I would see the woman's spirit again, but I never did. Yet, I always felt that house's eyes on me.

What began as a hopeful new beginning turned into a mockery of what life was supposed to be for my family.

I couldn't tell if Dad was genuinely happy or pretending for the sake of my sister and me. My sister and I were too young to understand what was happening with Dad. We have never lost twelve years of marriage or the love of our lives. We knew nothing of that kind of heartbreak.

I spent the final months of our lives in that house, feigning my way through.

I spent my Dad's assigned weeks waiting for the week to end. I ate dinners at the table, sometimes with Darlene there, sometimes not. I sat in the kitchen doing homework, begging God to stop me from looking up at the windows; sure, if I did, something unbearable would be peering back.

I endured the days that passed like years. I survived new school bullies that weren't half as bad as old school bullies.

My teacher liked me, sympathized with my familial situation, and was the first teacher I'd ever had to show patience with my ADHD. Still, I didn't excel particularly in his class, though I did achieve passing grades and even got an *E* for *Effort*.

I had friends, too. People I played with during recess, people who wanted to be around me. Even two girls in the class had a crush on me that would last throughout the fifth and sixth grades. Of course, nothing ever came of it. I was ten, but I wasn't willing to be teased by Mom or Dad for admitting anything about it.

I did my best in school, enjoyed my time at moms, and endured my time at Dad's. One week at a time, two weeks a month, I slept lightly on the couch with the television running and the volume low. I thank God that

Dad had cable. The last thing I wanted was to wake up to the national anthem and what followed. I'd rather fall asleep to *Nick-at-Night* and wake up to my favorite shows than to syndicated late-night reruns and wake up to television static.

I wasn't happy, but I pretended to be. I kept burying all that anger, all that pain and sorrow in my heart. I wandered through excruciating loneliness, enjoying the good things I could do and doing my best to be a good son to a mother I felt the need to protect and a father I begrudged.

All of that was going to change.

JUST ANOTHER DAY

Dad moved out of the house on West Grand in 1991 when the lease was up. With that hell hole behind us, it was a mixed blessing. Mom and Dad were officially divorced, and Dad was living with his girlfriend, Darlene, in a small condo in a small neighborhood. Stormy lived in their neighbor's gated yard, and the neighbor said we were always welcome to visit.

Darlene's house was small, maybe almost as small as Mom's apartment, but living with Darlene felt much more cramped. The couch folded into a bed, and that's where I slept. My sister slept in the only other bedroom in the house, which was a spare when Darlene's daughter Raquel wasn't visiting.

Darlene's house was dull. There was very little to do other than watch television or movies. The neighborhood was sparse, but a girl around my age lived across the way, and I hung out with her a few times before Dad told me to stop. When I asked why I had to stop, because I had no friends here, Dad explained that he didn't want to get to know the neighbors or have people coming over to Darlene's house because this would be temporary.

When I say nothing was going on, I mean *nothing*. There was nothing to do, nowhere to play, and I wasn't allowed to be friends with the only kid in the neighborhood my age. But it wasn't all bad. Other than sometimes having to watch the same movies repeatedly or do nothing at all, Dad had fun in a very hands-on way: parks, beaches, and theme parks. That was Dad's way whenever he could, but it was still dull.

Dad still dropped my sister and me off at the YMCA every morning, and they shuttled us to school and back. Dad would pick us up after work during his weeks with us much earlier than Mom would. The entire culture of *Dad-weeks* was different from *Mom-weeks*.

Mom-weeks meant friends could come and stay the night, or my sister and I could go and stay the night with our friends. During *Dad-weeks,* it was a neither-nor situation, where we couldn't go to friends' houses or have friends over. Dad was intent on it being his time with us, and that time should be spent as a family.

Dad was still angry with Mom, and I imagine Mom was still furious with Dad. The difference between the two was always a sharp contrast.

For example, our tiny apartment with Mom meant there was a swimming pool (two actually) available for tenants, and when we wanted to go swimming during

Dad-week, we could, but Darlene would come. Having Darlene in the same complex as Mom was uncomfortable, but angry Dad insisted that my sister and I drop our towels off at Mom's before we left and change clothes. Now, this part Mom knew was coming, and she was okay with it.

The part she wasn't aware of was that Dad wanted all of us to go upstairs together.

"Like a family," he'd said.

That's one of the pettiest, most childish plans he'd ever come up with, and even at ten, nearly eleven, I recognized it was a bad idea.

After swimming, I hurried my sister to Mom's house, where we dried off and changed clothes. When we found our Dad again, he was still at the pool with Darlene, and he was livid. How was Mom ever supposed to see that he was happy again and that we were delighted with Darlene?

Well, Dad was mistaken.

Happy as he may have been, we—my sister and I— were not, and while poor Darlene was just a pawn in the whole thing, the sweet woman was too willing to be a party to my dad's devices.

I, always looking to protect my mom back then, wasn't having it. I wasn't going to allow him to try to hurt my mom, even if it meant arguing with him. I would fight.

While I was thankful that I no longer had to worry about the danger the house on West Grand posed to my family, my father moving in with Darlene was not quite a step up. I was too angry back then to understand he was doing his best but carrying a lot of his own pain. It never excused the childish bullshit ideas he devised to hurt mom's feelings, but I understood Dad was a broken person with no idea how to be a grown adult man.

Things like that can be fixed, but broken people know that fixing requires a desire to be fixed. Getting better requires a willingness to get better and the ability to recognize there's a problem.

For Dad, it wasn't his fault; it was everybody else's fault—anyone else but him. That was the way his head worked; it was how he functioned. It was the only thing he knew, which must be a terrible and lonely way to live.

April came and went. I turned eleven. Music still hadn't quite figured out what it would be for the 1990s, though more and more people started wearing plaids and torn jeans. It wasn't something within my reach yet, something I didn't quite understand yet.

Then, one day, the shit hit the fan.

I can't tell you what that argument turned into a screaming match between a thirty-something-year-old man and his eleven-year-old son as we squared off in the parking lot in front of Darlene's apartments, but I can tell you I did not back down.

I dared him to hit me. I called him stupid for letting our family fall apart. I lost my mind, and I became completely unglued. I came apart at the seams—from all the pain, sorrow, and anger I'd jarred up since Mom and Dad split. All of it poured out in an avalanche that day.

He could have hit me if he had wanted to, pounded me into the pavement. He had made a feint, and I hadn't even flinched. I just kept staring him in the eyes, daring him to hit me if that's what he wanted to do.

I'd lost control and screamed in Darlene's face, screaming at both Raquel and my poor sister. The latter two were just casualties in the war I'd declared on my dad, but for Darlene, I told her I hated her and assured her it was not just a strong word but a promise.

My dad was the kind of man who started a battle, and when he'd calmed down, he would immediately regret his actions, his words, and anything he'd said or done. It was a life he knew growing up, the life I'd grown up with, watching how he and Mom fought.

He had been so heavy-handed with a belt when I was young, and the literal definition of crying over spilled milk—except he didn't cry. He got angry. He yelled. The man was a tyrant most of my life, but I was a child born under a tyrant who trusted and relied on him, who only understood that Dad was meant to love and provide safety. I didn't know until that day what kind of man my father was, or at least as an eleven-year-old, what kind of man I thought my father was or how I hated him.

I'd decided he was my enemy, but I was sure there would be no escape if I let him know. No reprieve. No respite. When he finally came to make up, I believed him. Of course, he was sorry. Of course, he loved me. Of course, he'd gone too far. We could make up, though. We could still be a family.

"Alright," I lied. "I forgive you."

The plan turned precision gears like clockwork in my head. I understood what I had to do, or my enemy would keep expecting me to come back, always to return. So, I lied some more. I told Dad I was homesick and wanted to return to my mom. He wasn't stricken. He was understanding.

Dad lost his mom when I was five, and I knew what the word *mother* meant to him. So, I played him. I demonstrated all the deceptions I'd believed he'd shown us my entire life. And it was true, I missed Mom. I wanted to go home, and he agreed, so I called home first and ensured she wasn't busy.

Mom okayed it because she's a mom. Mom could always tell by my tone of voice, cadence, or how I worded a sentence that something was wrong. She also knew my dad, and I grated on one another occasionally and that something was wrong if I asked to come home early.

Dad fell into the trap. He wanted a few more hours before I went home because he missed me. He apologized again, and I assured him he was forgiven.

He walked with my sister and me down to a corner liquor store, where he bought me peanut butter M&Ms.

We ate them as we walked back, and I expressed how happy I was that we made up. I hugged him and had to fight the urge to dig my knuckles into his kidneys because it was all I wanted to do. Find soft spots and break them. I swallowed back the anger, and we went back to Darlene's.

There would be a video recorder and a VHS tape inside it that I have no doubt my dad would watch from time-to-time following the period I went home.

I'm holding the camcorder so you can't see me, and it's aimed at his face.

I love you, daddy. I'm lying through my teeth, but for Dad, it's just his boy's voice and him returning with *I love you, too.*

Finally, it's time for him to take me home to my mom. My sister has chosen to stay, and that's fine. She was, at that time, daddy's girl. I had written an angry note while I waited for Dad to get his things—just a brief statement.

I lied. I hate you. I think you're stupid. I never want to see you again.

I hid it under the door handle to the sliding door on the side of the van. I jammed it under that handle in a way that I was sure it would never fall out. Then, as he approached the van, I climbed into the passenger seat as I had in 1988. He climbed into the driver's seat and started the van, and suddenly, my heart filled with grief.

The smell of Brut cologne was faint, but it was there, and we talked like old friends as he pulled out of the parking lot at Darlene's little condo complex and onto the street as he took me home.

When we got to the parking lot in front of my mom's, he asked if he could walk me up to the door, and I told him that I didn't think it was a good idea.

I lied that Mom was still hurt and angry, and that seemed to satisfy something inside him. We both got out and as I passed by the side panel door, I made sure the note was still there (it was). There was a part of me that wanted to forgive him and let it go, but if I did that, if I forgave him for this last battle if I let this go, he would only do it to me again and again.

Dad, in his stupid leather jacket, hugged me.

Stupid. So stupid. It's spring, the sun is out, the birds are chirping, and he's in a leather jacket.

He climbed back into his van and drove home.

I stood there in the parking lot, eleven years old. I felt older than I was, but I also just wanted to break down and cry to my dad and tell him how much I hated him because of how much I loved him, because of how badly he had let us all down. I couldn't do that now. There was no turning back. It was far too late. Eventually, he would pile into that van with Darlene, Raquel, and my sister. Someone would find that note, and Dad would see it.

I thought it would be closer to my sister's visitation, but it was much sooner than expected.

When I went inside, I was crying, and Mom was quick to my side. I told her everything: the fight, the hatred, and that I'd said and done terrible things. I told her how I had to lie to get away from my dad, how much I hated him (*oh, baby, you don't hate your dad*), and that I almost wanted him to die so I could be done with him so that he could leave us all alone.

Mom soothed me and tried to calm me, but I'd bottled that festering anger up since the summer of 1990, and it wasn't so easily assuaged, and I doubled down that I hated the man and not just for failing us. Dad had a mean streak; he was controlling and boring. I wasn't allowed to have friends or see the friends I did have. Dad was a monster, and I wasn't having any of Mom's peace talks.

The problem was I didn't truly feel that way. My heart kept breaking, and I already missed my dad. I wanted so badly to back down, but something new was happening inside me, something I couldn't let go of my pride. I refused to back down when I stood up to my dad, and I felt I had to stand by my decision not only not to see him again, but I had to hate him to ensure I stayed away.

I found ways to hate the man who had once been my hero. My life with him until the divorce played over and again through my head, even as older memories desperately tried to turn my point of view around, but I did what I thought I had to. I bottled the old memories up with my other painful feelings, and I buried them so deep that all I had left was anger.

The phone rang, and I felt cold blood in my veins.

He'd found the note.

Mom was on the phone, and her voice was *so* sympathetic.

No, John, he doesn't hate you. He's angry. He's just so angry. No, John. He doesn't want to talk to you; it's not a good time.

But Dad was persistent. Dad was losing his son, and it was breaking his heart. But I didn't see it that way. Dad was trying to get the upper hand. Dad was attempting to control me. He was trying to lord himself over me like I was some victim.

Dad did this to himself.

Everything else I've said until this point about hating Dad was a lie. I didn't hate my dad, but I couldn't force myself to release the anger. All I wanted was revenge. All I wanted was to punch the man, and I knew I was too small to fight him, too weak to beat him, and I loved him too much to do anything else but hate him. I hated knowing if I had to see him face-to-face again, I would fold.

Dad wanted to talk to me, *insisted* on talking to me, and as the courts deemed it, if he wanted to speak to me, Mom had to let him. She warned him and told him to let me cool down, but Dad would not relent.

Why, Dad? Why wouldn't you go away?

Mom handed me the phone.

I answered the phone as coldly as possible, "What do you want?"

My dad was a weak man hiding under a tyrant's veneer. He was a broken child trapped in a man's body, a child who'd been beaten by his father, loved by his mother—but not loved so much that she was ever willing to leave the man who hit her child—and he had no idea how to be a real person. His voice was so stricken on the phone, so caught in his throat. Dad was a stutterer.

If you ever wanted to know if my dad had reverted into a grief state, you waited for the stutter. How cruel is it for me to say at eleven years old, I had beaten and broken my father? How evil was it that I reveled in the power I felt over him? How was I to know, the state I was in, that I had become as much of a monster as he had? How could he love me now? How could I love him, the fucking traitor who ruined my family and destroyed everything?

No, go to hell, John. That is what I wanted to say, but I didn't.

I let him stutter over his voice, explain how he thought we'd made up and how I promised we were okay. I allowed him to run on until his voice trailed off.

I lied. I lied to get away from you. I lied because I don't love you. I hate you. I hate you!

b--but I --I M-M-Michael...

I mocked his stutter back to him, laughed, and hung the phone up hard enough that I knew he heard it.

Mom was on me immediately, furious that I had just mocked my father. Maybe Mom and Dad couldn't get along; maybe they couldn't be married; perhaps it was over between them, *but Michael is your father.*

No, I didn't care. I lied to her. I lied to myself. Those lies we tell ourselves to hide from the things that scare us. I was as frightened about the things pouring out of my mouth as any of the evil things lurking in that old house, that creaking, shifting, hateful place.

Then, I broke down and started crying. I felt weak from breaking down. I felt like my entire world was shattered, but I wept about how much I hated my dad. I cried in my mother's embrace, and she said nothing at all. I'm not sure if she didn't know what to say or knew to say nothing at all; I'm not sure if the unwritten parenting rules had an answer for this.

Suppose you're a father in any capacity. I hope you never have to go through this. If you're a father of broken children from a broken home, I'm so sorry you must go through that, and I'm sorry for your kids. I'm a father.

My eldest adopted me when she was six, and my two biological children have always been there. Even after the divorce, they stuck by me, and I did my best to be the best father I could be. Nothing is more complicated than helping your children navigate the aftermath of a hard-weathered storm.

I cannot fathom what it would feel like if any of my three children hated me or even just said they hated me. I cannot comprehend what I did to my father, in part because I am a better father than he was but also because there are things you cannot understand unless you experience them yourself.

I can tell you there are times when I fear in secret that any one of my children will say to me to my face, or through a phone, or worse, a text. Fear in secret that one or all of them will tell me someday that they never want to see me again. What could I do? What could I say to change their mind? I look back on the little boy I was at eleven, and if my children are anything like I was, there is nothing in that moment I could do but be completely destroyed by it.

That's what I did to John, the safest person on earth to me, once upon a time: my hero, buddy, and best pal as a child. I had taken someone who had *always* been willing to play, even when he was exhausted from work, troubled, or sad—even after his mother died when I was five—a man who could put on a brave face and appreciate the love of his son and daughter.

We don't cry outwardly. It was the way I was raised. Never let anyone who could use your heart against you see a moment of weakness. I've never wept at a funeral, never shed a tear in public. I've never shown an ounce of that sorrow in a classroom setting, in my childhood at the YMCA, or anywhere else to follow.

There is a place for it, in the company of a loved one, in your room where no one else can see. Tears are shared in private with family. I was raised to understand that children must only ever see the strong side of a parent, never know despair or fear, always see the best of their parents, and never the worst.

It doesn't always work out that way, but I'm not ashamed to admit that I've stared at my daughters and my son, and I've grieved for what I did to that man, and I remember that an angry eleven-year-old boy destroyed a grown man with a few horrible words, mocked him and broke him because he could.

In the entirety of my life up until that point, Dad had rarely stuttered. It happened after his mom died, but even then, that was it. I feel guilt for what I did to that man. I mourn When I think of what I did to ensure he always knew I hated him. Dad wouldn't want me to carry that guilt, and I know that, but when I think of what he did, I sometimes get angry. Dad was the type of man who was a terrible father in his prime, but the kind of fun most grandparents could only wish they were.

No more Brut Cologne, I'm sorry to say.

No more special late nights or father-son secret silent trips to breakfast.

I put my dad behind me and trampled my way through the following years of my life, bearing the pain in my heart and soul, and buried myself in fury and anger. Whenever I felt guilt, sympathy, empathy, or mercy for the man, I would remind myself who I thought he was.

This persisted through the years. I was eleven, but then I was eleven, no more. Grade school turned into Junior High. My sister stopped seeing him, though her reasons were her own. Dad finally got his wish. All the travel and all the world, all the time he wanted as often as he wanted with his new bride, Darlene, and so he finally left.

I was not alright. I was not better.

I still had bullies in junior high, and I learned that they were a part of life for everyone at one point or another.

My legacy in self-defense had been forgotten here, so I established on more than one occasion that I may be willing to allow them to talk, but putting hands on me was a mistake. The problem was now, though, placing hands on me wasn't met with equal force—it was met with relentless force.

The first half of my seventh-grade year was most often punctuated with a fight during lunch or P.E. I either won or the fights were a draw. Still, as the year progressed, my peripheral associations became allies and eventually friends.

Before the year would close, I'd made friends with the right people. I employed no short amount of creativity to ensure that anyone who made the mistake of crossing me would meet both physical punishment and more underhanded punishments (insomuch that absence and tardy slips mysteriously disappeared before they could get to the school administration, and more than a few attempted bullies ended up in detention, Saturday school, or suspended).

The bullying stopped. Completely.

Life was improving. We were now living in a house in the Home Gardens area of Corona, California. My dad was quite literally on the other side of the world, and I just kept burying his memory whenever I began to miss him.

AN AUTUMN DAY IN 1992

It was a rainy Friday afternoon in the Autumn of 1992 when the phone rang. A phone was in the den, the kitchen, and the living room. I'd been expecting a call from one of my friends about what the evening would bring, whether we would see a movie or go out and do something. I had no idea Dad would be on the other side of that call when I answered the phone. It had only been a year, but it felt like ten, and despite missing Dad, a sudden well of anger rose in me, and I hung up.

But Dad called back and pleaded with me not to hang up again. I told him I did not want to talk to him, and he asked my mom. Mom must have heard me from the other room because she was already in the den, reaching for the phone and chastising me for being disrespectful.

When I see myself in my mind's eye, I want to throttle that kid. That disrespectful punk ignored his mom; I ignored my mom. I told Dad he needed to hurry up, and I was waiting for an important call. I tossed the phone to the floor. I went back to playing the Super Nintendo, which, ironically, my dad had given my sister and me through a Christmas he hadn't been around for. It's a strange kind of hypocrisy when you can hate someone for simultaneously being around and not being around.

Then I heard Mom asking, *what do you mean you're dying?*

I lost my head at that moment and began yelling at her, telling her to hang up on the man and let him die already.

Mom was making furious eyes at me, and I was ignoring her anger and telling her to hang up on the dumb bastard. I knew he could hear me, and I knew if he heard how little I cared about whether he lived or died, it would hurt him. I wanted to inflict pain as deeply as I could.

Except I didn't want that at all, but I couldn't stop myself.

Why hadn't he fought harder, demanding with a police escort and the full force of the courts that I visit him during his assigned visitation? Why did he move to Indonesia to work, leaving my sister and me behind?

When you're that angry, that hurt, when you're a kid, and you've run out of reasons to hate someone, you find yourself making excuses. That's when you may find yourself driving people off and hating them for leaving, telling them not to call or write, and then hating them for their silence.

Dad had a blood pathogen the doctors hadn't seen before, and on top of that, he had dysentery. When you take vacations, you hear there are some places where you're just not supposed to drink the water or do whatever Dad did to get sick.

Mom then yelled at Dad. She demanded he fix his situation and get healthy. See, that wasn't anger. That was fear. I did not know Mom would love Dad for the rest of her life. It's just that, like so many things, adult life isn't idyllic.

Sometimes, love isn't enough.

Fortunately, Dad didn't die. I hated him a little less for that and was secretly relieved.

It was not enough to talk to or see him, but the world still had him in it, and for now, that was enough for me.

EASTER, 1995

It is strange how only four years felt like ten without my father in them. Even as an adult, I feel like I hadn't spoken to him for a decade before the phone rang in our new apartment in the Meadowood Villas. I was fifteen years old when my mom answered the phone that afternoon, stood in stunned silence for a moment, and then handed me the phone with a cautious intonation. *It's your father.*

Hey, Dad, what's up?

Dad was quiet, too. If he was careful not to immediately trust the pleasant nature of my voice at that moment, he was right.

After all, only four years earlier, I had run the most extensive, darkest, coldest deception a child could and had done the most wicked thing a son could do to his father. Then, as though he'd shaken off thoughts I could only speculate, he informed me he was in California for Easter and had news: my father's long-deceased half-brother had kids, new cousins for me to meet, and they sought a reunion of epic proportions.

Would I want to go to a family Easter with him?

Mom was the one who wasn't receptive, but in the end, recognizing I was willing to go with my dad to spend time with him and meet new family, she relented. Not only she but my sister, too. We were both going to meet our newfound family.

This is, in my life, one of the most beautiful moments I would ever experience. Dad pulled up in his rented car, got out, and greeted me. My sister was still moments away, getting a few things before she would arrive.

My dad got out of the car and walked up to me, and I offered him my hand for a handshake, and holy shit, that man was just as strong as I remember. Three things happened when he brushed my hand out of the way and pulled me into an embrace. First, I hugged him back harder than I'd ever in a giant bearhug.

I had to fight back tears because I missed him so much. All the pain, all the hate, all the anger left me just as my breath left my lungs with the strength of his hug. Next, he was a couple of inches shorter than I. I'd grown so much since the day we stood toe-to-toe, our fists balled as though we were going to throw fists at one another. Finally, I noticed that as strong as he was, he felt light and small.

I whispered an apology and let go of years of pride and pent-up anger, but he'd already forgiven me.

I forgave you immediately, Michael. The day it happened.

It was a good reunion, more so amazing that strangers you'd never met in your entire life could be so much like you. I can't discuss much of it, some of that being that it has no bearing on the story and other bits being that it's just too painful. It was just a beautiful reunion. It was better because Dad was there, and I was there with Dad.

CHRISTMAS, 1995

Dad was there yet again in the Christmas season of 1995. He had a brush with death but saw the light and found faith in faith healers (despite there being several different media outlets that had exposed 'faith healers' to be a sham), and in his most recent near-terminal illness, he had been healed completely. He had been saved an inch from death, and he'd gotten remarried. He insisted this would be his third and final marriage.

I feel so bad for having found relief in this, but Darlene was the final link in a chain that bound me to the pain of a divorce six years ago.

Dad met some of my friends this time, and he and I played guitar together. No, that's a lie. He played guitar phenomenally well, and I clumsily strummed an acoustic like a novice, but Dad loved that his son loved guitar classic rock. He looked at me with the same expression, marveling at me as though I were the strangest and most exciting creature he had ever seen.

You know, when I look through old photos of me as a baby, he and I are dressed identically in almost all of them.

Hah, and Dad still wore Brut. Older people are static beings stuck in their ways. It was perfect.

Oh, and something happened that had not occurred for years. We went to our new cousin's house, where we spent Christmas Eve with other new family members I hadn't known about. We ate good food and opened gifts. Then, Dad drove us to Grandma and Grandpa Denny's for the first time in six years, and we spent the remainder of Christmas Eve there.

It felt real. These things that hadn't happened in so long fell back into place, but because they so quickly fell into step, I kept waiting for the other boot to drop. When was Dad going to yell? When would we next stand face to face, ready to fight, and would we throw fists?

Except, this time, it didn't happen. Something changed in Dad, and I imagine part of it was that I didn't live with him, and part of it, I believe, was the realization that his actions had real consequences.

I don't know. The topic never came up, but the other boot never dropped, at least not as far as us being miserable, locked in another blowout fight. Dad never once raised his voice to me, never yelled at me, and he spent much more time asking me what I wanted than telling me what I would do. He was old and new and the same and changed all at once.

It was not so changed that he still worked out of state, but at least now he lived in the states.

A RETURN TO MY ROOTS

The year 1996 brought so many different things. I'd left home after several arguments with Mom. I was an incorrigible teenager, less grateful than I should have been and far more willful than I had the right. Mom and my relationship had been strained at times, but I opted to stay with a friend. During that time, I began having nightmares again. This time, that leathery flesh and hollow gaze reached for me from behind the door's shadow.

I was no stranger to dreams of the house on West Grand, and as I've said, most of my life was peppered with those nightmares, haunted by a house that I no longer haunted. The more I ignored the nightmares, the more they came.

It was a strange thing, then, that Dad should return in the Spring of 1997. I was on Spring Break, with Easter on the Horizon, and relished my time with him.

He didn't even have a problem with my friend Allen coming along. During this strange period, I'd confided some of this story in Allen, the house, the woman behind the door, the Bloody Mary, and the nightmares that came with it.

One afternoon, on our way to my aunt's house in Norco, California, I asked my dad: *What weren't you telling me about the house on West Grand?*

I could swear all day long that the temperature in the car dropped a few degrees, but that was just in my head. Dad was quiet for a bit. I doubt he'd spared much thought to the topic of that old house, the house always watching, always breathing, always hungry, no less talked about it at any length. Yet, at its mention, the hairs on his arms stood up straight, and there was gooseflesh. Then, nervous laughter.

Geez, man. Look at my arms.

Dad discussed a little, denying having experienced anything himself, except that Darlene had seen the woman sitting on her side of the bed. He remembered. He told me that the house was always kind of weird to him, but he'd never experienced anything himself. My mom, and of course my sister and I, sure. But not him. Never him. He became very evasive as we pulled into a gas station. As he went inside to pay for some fuel, my friend Allen tapped me on the shoulder from the back seat.

You know he's hiding something, right? He seems like he's hiding something.

Of course, Allen was right, though Dad would hold his position that he'd experienced nothing. He would tell tales of his mom and her mom and how they were a little bit *sensitive* to things around them, could sense things and feel things that weren't normally in reach, and that he'd always worried that some of that would catch on my sister, or me, or both of us.

Dad did confess as much that, at times, he was unnerved by the house, and though he insisted he never saw anything, he always felt something. He always felt like he was being watched. He never went into the root cellar alone.

There was still so much I wanted to know, but it was clear that Dad wouldn't relent any further. So, I let it go. Dad took Allen and me to a small local theme park with miniature golf and an arcade, and we enjoyed the day. I did not bring the house on West Grand up to him again.

Dad's visits were always too short, but at least he lived in Connecticut now. I could call without adjusting for international time zones. Not that we did much calling, but it was indeed available, and besides that, Dad said he'd be back to visit in the summer.

After Dad's visit, after he returned to Connecticut, I didn't so easily give up. I walked to the house on West Grand only to find no one was home. I couldn't be sure anyone lived there, though I was incredibly uncomfortable near it. The house on its own, in broad daylight, was quiet, and for lack of a better way to say this, it didn't seem to notice I was there.

That should sound so wild to me now. The inanimate object that had sat in the same spot since 1916 was unaware I was near it. It would sound unbelievable to me now had I not occupied its space for two years, been afraid of its root cellar and whatever lurked behind its doors. I did not attempt to go to the door and knock or tour the property. The longer I was there, the longer I didn't want to be there.

I would drive by the place a couple more times with a friend to see if anyone was home, but clearly, it wasn't the time. My questions, however burning in me they may be, would have to wait because no one had answers.

I spent my year waiting for Dad to return at the Corona Public Library in the historical archives, looking for anything I could. There was so much on many of Corona's historical properties but nothing about the house. No blueprints. There is no history other than it had been built in 1916. No pictures. No distant owners. No architect. No designer.

No one. Nothing.

The history of that horrible place has been lost entirely, and I could not locate anyone who knew anything further back than the last owners. I failed to find anything more than I already did.

If you'd asked me back then why I was so studious about this house, this terrible place, I couldn't have told you why. I couldn't have expressed my longing in words or even the sick desire to move back into the house if only to study it.

Inside the walls of that house, I believed it was a horrendous evil, but not only that; every bad memory every occupant ever had seemed locked in its walls; every misery or even tragedy absorbed into that old place as though it not only fed on the analogical emotional bile, but I believed it kept them. I believed it kept them like trophies, a place whose immaterial occupation by some damned entity collected bad memories and replayed them on top of its derisive malice.

It was not the goal of this thing or things inside that house to scare people. It wanted the screaming, the fighting, and the mental and emotional violence; it wanted dissent and destruction, and then, like some sick highlight reel, it desired that to happen repeatedly, so long as its bound structure should stand.

As he promised, Dad returned. He came back to us for Christmas of 1996. Like the year before, we Christmas hopped from his side of the family—a family he'd lost and regained in his lifetime. He brought Maria Oka, my stepmother, the last woman he swore to me that he would ever marry.

For Dad, that was a big deal. I was only sixteen then, but I could see that the man had changed a great deal and grown up quite a bit from the man I'd fought with when I was eleven.

There was no other boot, and that defensive pride he'd held onto for so long was just gone. He'd grown or gotten tired of being angry so much. Maybe he'd realized life was too short for fighting, with this latter part being the most authentic conjecture at the time but a fact in the making all the same.

Dad met Maria in the Philippines after he and Darlene hadn't worked out. The two got along famously.

Given Dad and Maria's faith, all of Dad's previous marriages were annulled through the church and, in the eyes of the church itself, never existed. He married Maria, and the two were happy. I was glad for Dad.

Maria wasn't intrusive in my or my sister's life and seemed adamant to be helpful if we needed it, but she stayed on the sidelines unless we asked her for help.

To this end, I liked Maria. I appreciated the fact that she was personable and well-spoken. She was only eight years older than me, but most importantly, she and Dad seemed to be one another's checks and balances. Dad said he didn't drink except for these family parties and never to get drunk; he'd given up all drugs when he was faced with the decision to either keep up the party life or lose Maria.

I was relieved. It was about time. He was getting his priorities straight and putting his heart where it belonged, not in some rock and roll pipe dream. Things couldn't have been better then unless he had moved back to California so I could see him more often.

The thought at the time was shocking to me, a revelation that I'd gone from trying my hardest to hate my dad to wishing he was closer and rebuilding a relationship with him—not at a pace he demanded—but at a pace that I was comfortable—building and rebuilding trust.

I couldn't have told you a damned thing about what catalyst caused such a dramatic amount of change in such a short period back then, but I can now tell you it wasn't anything I saw coming.

A FAMILY AFFAIR

The strangest thing happened to me between Christmas of 1996 and May of 1997 because that was as long as it took for me to see my dad again.

Addressing this, it wasn't his fault this time. It was mine. He'd asked my sister and me to visit him in Connecticut and even offered to pay for the plane flight, but we'd refused. He'd explained how beautiful it was, how lovely it was in just about every season.

Still, we refused. He protested a bit and explained that we didn't travel enough (always with Dad, travel, but he was right), and we said we didn't want to go there, but maybe another time. Dad relented, which continued to surprise me. In retrospect, I do wish I'd gotten to see the Connecticut countryside.

Dad wrote us letters by mail, neglecting email altogether, and I'd write back (much shorter letters). Finally, in the Spring of 1997, Dad came home.

Dad didn't even mention it. My sister and I climbed into his car and went to our cousin's. We stayed there for dinner and spent the entire time catching up with our family and one another. Dad talked to me, adamant that I would come to see him in Connecticut, and finally, I relented, expressing that it did sound like a great idea.

For all the excitement of the day, I couldn't tell you what happened, you know? I hung out with my cousins, my second cousins, Dad, uncles, and aunts. Dad dropped a major bomb on us. *Tomorrow*, he said to us, *Disneyland*.

I was beside myself. I'd been going there for my birthday every year since I was twelve. There was so much Dad hadn't seen since my childhood that he'd missed. The excitement was unbearable. How would I manage to sleep?

I woke up to something I had never experienced, and it was weird to me. Not a bad weird, but weird all the same. I woke to my dad petting my goatee. Well, what passes for a goatee for a seventeen-year-old. A tuft of fine brow hair on my chin that passed for facial hair.

He was staring at me in a way I'd never seen him stare, and his eyes were brimming. I asked him if everything was okay, and he insisted that seeing me with facial hair was just so odd.

Hah. Facial hair. It looked like I'd rubbed dirt on my chin, but all my friends had goatees, and we'd all grown ours out for reasons I can't even remember, but I imagine we thought it made us look older.

Then the day began, and we met with his brother, my uncle, at Disneyland, where we spent the entirety of the day. Halfway through the day, my uncle was tired and went home, leaving Dad, my sister, and me to explore the park together. I showed him all the rides that weren't there when we used to go as small kids and all the rides they'd removed since then. By the end of the day, Dad, my sister, and I were exhausted as it grew dark.

We found our way back into the tram to the parking lot and climbed back into his car. Dad drove us back to Corona, dropping my sister off at home and me in the apartment complex where I would meet my friends that evening.

We said farewell, and I asked if he'd be around for Christmas. Dad promised he'd get there if he could but stated that work was hectic, and he had to meet deadlines. I believed him because Dad was a changed man, but Dad was lying. Dad wasn't coming for Christmas that year. He was lying but not maliciously.

I am thankful for May of 1997. After our brief conversation, I hugged him. I was taller than Dad by four inches now, and that was with him in cowboy boots. Still, he picked me up, the man wearing a leather jacket (though I no longer saw it as a stupid leather jacket), and kissed my face like a toddler, and I could smell his Brut cologne. Dad was safe again. His hair was thinning, and there were abundant patches of gray.

Without stopping myself, I told him: *I love you, Daddy.*

Daddy. I hadn't uttered that word since I was small, but I'm glad I did.

It was the last time I would ever see him alive.

THE UN–FOND FAREWELL

I t's unsettling to me the sudden and rapid decline of Dad's health. When we said our farewells in late May of 1997, Dad had to have known he was sick. There's no way he could not because he was dead by June 23, 1997, four days after his forty-first birthday.

Dad didn't get to die in Connecticut, though. At some point during his decline, he returned to the Philippines to see his faith healer, but there was no saving him.

My last conversation with my dad was me talking to him because he couldn't talk to me with a tube down his throat. I cannot translate into words the devastation I felt as I spoke to him on the phone, like my world wasn't crashing around me. Again. I won't even try.

No, I told him I was okay, would be alright, and loved him. I promised him I would take care of my mom and my sister, and he could rest and go home, and I'd see him again one day. I said whatever I could to put his heart at ease, and he choked back a gurgling sound.

It was June 18, 1997, after our final phone call, that I realized it isn't only the lies we tell ourselves when we're afraid. It's the lies we tell others to alleviate their fears, too. I didn't say this to save my hide; this wasn't even a frightful experience. I'd spent my entire life until that moment fearing that one or both of my parents would die before their time, and for my dad, his time was nearly up. We were past the point of my fears, and all I wanted for him was some peace.

In the end, what mattered was that Dad didn't leave. Dad came back. Dad returned and made peace with me, with everyone around him that he could.

Ultimately, I saw who loved my dad when bitterness fell by the wayside.

When I'd said what I said to Dad on the phone, Mom took the phone.

John, you can't give up. You've always been a fighter, and you need to fight this. You need to get better. You must get out of this.

They divorced only seven years prior, and maybe they weren't in love, but Mom loved Dad. He was the father of her children, and there was something else. In all my life, I'd only seen Mom and Dad, never the people they were beneath the titles. I'd never imagined who they were before I was born or before they were married; I'd never even asked what it was like when they were dating.

For me, Dad was dying. For Mom, John was dying. John, who she'd met through her mother. John, who she'd disliked at first, whose notorious charm worked its way through. John, who started a life with her. For Mom, it was 12 years of marriage and two children, and she knew that, yes, John was a fighter, strong, and he wasn't someone who just gave up, but this time, Mom was wrong.

It was time for Dad to lay down his arms, put away his fight, and rest. He'd made a hard life for himself and had chosen a hard road. Ultimately, he made right with anyone he could, and he would leave the world a good man.

On June 22, 1997, I went to stay with my cousins, my previously lost relatives who were invested in my dad, my sister, and me as though we'd always been family. We discussed funeral arrangements where and how we would set up a service for my father.

Dad died on June 23, 1997. I was sleeping when it happened, and the news came to me from his half-sister, a phone call in the early morning hours.

Michael, he's gone. Johnny's gone.

We mourned as a family, all except me. I was heartbroken, but while one side of the family was all about feeling, *no one* would see me cry. No one was allowed to.

I would never reveal weakness in public because that's how I was raised. I would be stoic at Dad's funeral, which would be roughly a week later. His remains had to be shipped back to the United States from the Philippines. We had the funeral, and then it was over. Grandpa Oka held the wake, and we held fellowship with our family, remembering Dad and honoring his memory.

Then, I did something I was not supposed to do. I did the same things I did when I was an angry child, and I buried the pain. I lied to myself that I was alright, and that Dad was gone, and because he was gone—because there was nothing that I could do about it—that I would just let it go. The thing is, I didn't let it go. I had to constantly distract myself with anything I could to keep myself from slipping into misery. It would have been easier to mourn, but I refused. I can't even tell you why I declined.

Dad's death was painful for me but not as heartbreaking as it would have been had he and I not made amends and new memories before his passing. Dad's return was one of the biggest blessings in my life.

One of my favorite memories is of my dad, shorter than me, picking me up in that apartment parking lot and kissing me on the face, smelling of his Brut cologne in his not-so-stupid leather jacket.

I felt so much guilt for such a long time for the time I wasted as a child pushing Dad away. I think that hit me as hard as Dad's passing, but Mom (being a parent) told me that I was only a child, that my dad understood that and had forgiven me long before I apologized. She also reminded me that in putting the past behind us, I'd given my dad his son back before he passed, and that was all my dad would have wanted.

The kind things we say to one another, to calm the mind, the heart, the soul; the niceties are always kinder if they're true. Back then, I had no idea if what Mom said was the truth. I was seventeen and had no kids of my own.

At forty-two, with three children of my own, I finally understand. There is nothing I would not do for my children. There is nothing I would not forgive. They have their anger, too. My youngest is the most vocal about it, and while I am sad that he is so upset about his parents divorcing—because I never wanted that for them.

I am relieved that he and my other two children are willing to discuss it with me. The things that bother them. The difficulty of visitation. I can relate to them.

I am glad my children want me to live, urge me to get regular checkups, and they're happy to see me alive. They express their sorrow, anger, and disappointment, and we talk and work it out. I wish I'd had the strength to do that myself as a child.

It wasn't until November of 1998, standing at my Grandpa Denney's deathbed, that I finally understood something from the year before. Grandpa was dying, so I didn't expect him to move as fast as he did when he reached for the collar of my shirt and pulled me close to him.

I thought he was going to say something profound, and in a way, he did. Grandpa got me by the collar of my shirt, and for a dying man, he was strong. He pulled me close and reached out with his other hand; he patted the poor excuse for a beard on my face and *smiled*.

All at once, I understood. He'd held me when I was an infant, spoiled me as a little boy, and treated me like I was a man by the time I was fifteen.

He was kind and empathetic following the death of my father, but here at his bedside, a dying older man reached out and stroked what I thought passed for a beard, and it took me back for a moment to May of 1997, waking up to my father petting that dirt patch on my chin that I called a goatee.

For Grandpa Denney, his baby grandson was grown up. Crappy beard and all. For Dad, his baby boy had grown up. It confirmed to me that Dad knew he was dying and that it was probably his last trip to see his kids and his family.

Grandpa would have told me to shave any other day of my life. He would have informed me I looked disheveled. There, on his deathbed, a grandpa said goodbye not to his baby grandson but from one man to another.

I think about that a lot, both grandpa and Dad. Bittersweet memories, one I didn't understand until the other happened, and then it was something indelibly marked in my memories.

I look at my kids, and I see the babies I hold. One day, my little boy will have a ratty mustache, goatee, or a wiry beard. He'll feel like a grown-up. I understand what my dad was saying. I know Grandpa's goodbye.

In our children, we pass a torch when it's time to go, hoping their lives are infinitely better.

I don't know how my dad's last moments were. I know what killed him, but I don't know how he died. I know how he lived, though. For all his failures, Dad did right by as many people as he could at the end of his life.

In the end, he died a father and not a stranger. I can live with that.

RETURNING TO THE SCENE

It was early afternoon on Saturday, October 27, 2001, while cruising the Corona, California boulevard, when my friend and I ended up on West Grand. On impulse, and for no reason I could tell you, I convinced my friend that we should stop in my old neighborhood. I hadn't been there—had actively avoided the property—in a long time.

Dad was dead for four years now, and I think maybe I just wanted a touchstone.

We pulled up and parked alongside the house and exited the car. I'd taken some time to give him some backstory on the house before pulling up to the property, though we weren't prepared for more than a quick look.

The afternoon sun was obscured by a few clouds, the seasonal weather just right for the day. I led my friend alongside the house, pointing to the window where my room was when my sister and I first moved into the house. I took him to the driveway where Dad used to park his van, and a woman was standing on the porch.

It was an awkward silence for a few moments before she asked if she could help me. I introduced myself and my friend and explained that I used to live there and was visiting old memories. I was surprised at her thoughtful expression. She broke the silence with a question that still sends me chills when I think about it.

When you lived here, did anything strange ever happen?

Mine wasn't an immediate answer. You don't just walk up to a stranger and start panicking them with dark tales of the macabre. Especially if their idea of strange and your concept of strange don't align. I asked what she meant by *strange* because that seemed like the right question.

...but of course, I knew what she meant.

I knew she would ask me about the house or something in it, and she did. She asked if my family had heard anything or felt like the house was strange.

At this point, I think she and I were both confident the other wouldn't believe us crazy, so I told her that strange things did happen in my experience for the two years I was in the house—strange, inexplicable things.

There was some hesitation. Why not? I was just some guy trying to get into her house for all she knew. I offered some proof and told her that in her garage, on the wall farthest from the door, in the back above the worktable, there would be two bumper stickers on the wall featuring the U.S. Navy's Blue Angels. I explained that my dad had been a fan of the Blue Angels and that the bumper stickers would still be there unless they removed them.

She said she hadn't ever noticed anything like that in the garage, and I offered to show her. I expected she would tell me no, maybe thank me for my time. Maybe not. Then, that would be it.

That's not what happened. She said I could show her, so I had my friend wait by the gate while I went into her backyard, opened the door to the garage—turned the light on because I knew where the light switch was—and led her to the work bench. There on the wall were my father's Blue Angels bumper stickers.

She was surprised. Not she or anyone else in her household had ever looked around the garage. They didn't use it for their car. A few boxes were stored in it, but they didn't go in the garage.

Once we were back in the front yard, I told her the layout of her house, from the concrete steps, through the kitchen into the living room; from the living room, the den next to it; the hallway, to the left a master bedroom, in the middle a restroom and toward the end to the right, two additional bedrooms. One to the left, next door to the bathroom, and one door straight into the second largest room.

If she needed convincing, I imagine that was all it took. She was making pleasantries, but I'd been distracted by the yard. Nothing had changed. The orange tree was still there, the pomegranate bush.

This was where my sister and I played with our friends. This had been where we played with Stormy once upon a time. I remember feeling such a mixture of bittersweet memories of our time in that yard. For Robert and Jessica, Erica, and Jessie, and how fast and fleeting my once present became the past.

She asked me if my friend and I would like to come inside and maybe I could answer any questions they might have.

I agreed but paused at the bottom of those large concrete stairs. I was going to set foot inside the house again, and there was a heavy, sinking feeling in my stomach. It was that falling feeling, that red flag warning system. It was the same feeling from childhood: prey, perilously close to the predator, hiding in the brush. I felt a sensation of recognition, like, *oh, I remember* you.

Still, with my friend in tow, I ascended those concrete steps and entered the kitchen.

I wonder if people are more alike than they realize. Their kitchen table, while not the same as ours had been, was set precisely where ours was when I lived there. Four seats at a round table situated only a few feet from the door.

As we entered the kitchen, she introduced us to her son, a younger man, maybe about sixteen or seventeen, standing at an ironing board, ironing a thick black jacket. He politely acknowledged us for a moment and returned to ironing his coat.

We passed through the kitchen into the living room, and it was like stepping back in time. Their entertainment center was situated where ours had been, their couch along the same wall where my family sat for family movie nights on Sundays. The only thing missing was a coffee table and a rocking chair by the half-wall dividing the living room from the den, but they had a computer desk and a computer in the den.

The woman introduced me to her father, who lounged on the couch. We shook hands, and he asked about our business there. I didn't have to answer. The kind lady did it for me. She explained my prior residence there and that I had also experienced strange things— the man on the couch, her father, visibly relaxed. He didn't just relax, though. He looked so relieved.

It's such a strange thing to exist in a vacuum. Everyone seems to have ghost stories or a house they lived in where they lived with the weird, the unknown, and the unexplained. These aren't things you talk about often, except in hushed whispers, in quiet corners with your family, closest friends, and most trusted confidants. Everyone seems to have a story, but no one wants to share it. No one likes to be branded crazy, so you live with that secret. You keep it because it keeps you, and you endure it until it stops, you move, or you move on.

My friend and I stood in the living room where the window once rattled as the blinds shook at the challenge of my mom. The same horizontal blinds I knew as a child were covered in a thin layer of dust. I half expected to see a stripe down one side where an unseen finger once ran down from the top to the bottom at my mother's ill-planned challenge. Of course, it wasn't there, and if it had been, I'd have left right then and there.

So, dad-on-the-couch asked me what I'd experienced there, and I countered with the same question. I clarified that I wanted to compare their experiences to my own rather than influence any experiences they had with my own.

He explained that he had never seen anything but heard plenty and often. Footsteps from the kitchen to the hall. The sound of two children running and playing through the house: a girl and a boy.

I didn't say anything, but his experience took my imagination to a dark place, some secret horror inside me that the house had taken enough from my family that it replayed for them the sounds of my sister and I playing; that somehow, we'd left enough behind, like the phosphorescent hobo from 1984, a moment in the house recorded, and played again and again for all to hear.

He explained that he slept on the couch in the living room, his wife having passed only a couple of years prior.

He said there were times when the house didn't feel safe, or he felt like someone, or something, was watching him.

Hearing this made telling my side of the story much more difficult because the last thing I wanted to do was scare anyone or make them uncomfortable in their own home.

Still, I was assured by both the kindly woman who invited us in and her father that it was something they were already wrestling with as a family.

So, I told the truth. When I lived there, I was eight, nine, and ten before moving out, and I'd never heard the little girl and boy playing in the house, but I'd heard footsteps before, from under the house in the root cellar (*we never go into the root cellar, we keep it locked*).

I shared my mom's experience in the living room the night she came home from work. I explained the window and the blinds, and after that, she'd had our dog Stormy do a quick run-through every night, and since he'd said they never go into the root cellar, I assured him nothing was exciting down there worth seeing.

The lady who let us in called her daughter out. She was in her late teens, maybe eighteen or nineteen. Unlike her brother, still ironing his coat in the kitchen, she was happy to talk to me. She slept in the room where my sister saw The Bloody Mary, and though she never actually saw anything herself, she'd still had experiences.

She explained the sensation of being watched or in danger and of something unknown close to her. She could hear it breathe. The breathing I'd never heard as a child. Something close whose presence wasn't just heard but felt in my ear? Never. Not once, but for her, it happened often.

She said this happened sometimes when she showered, sometimes when she was in her room, alone— the sensation that she was not alone and the sound of something breathing near her ear.

Finally, their mom—the kind lady who let us in— explained that she saw a shadow in her room from time-to-time, something standing at the foot of her bed, in a corner, or in front of the closet (which she kept closed).

The mother said she could sometimes see a shadow in her room, the same room that had been my mom and dad's. She stated she heard footsteps through the house when such sounds had no business being there; she heard the children playing and breathing in her ear. She said if one room in the house made her particularly uncomfortable, it was the kitchen.

Of all the places she felt were being watched, she said the kitchen she sensed the most, as though something was peering in from those six high windows.

After she and her daughter shared their experiences, I asked first if they were confident. They wanted to hear what I had to say. I didn't want to leave them with stories that couldn't be unsaid, but they insisted.

I shared my experience with the woman behind the door, my sister's experience with what she called the bloody Mary, and my dad's girlfriend seeing the woman in the master bedroom, sitting motionless on the side of his bed. I told them how my dog Stormy reacted to something we couldn't see. When I was done, I had one favor to ask.

Finally, and I guess what would be inevitable, I asked about the root cellar. They kept it locked and said they didn't go down there or even use it for storage.

I asked if I could go in, and they were quiet, hesitant for a moment, but agreed I could. So, the kind lady led us outside. She unlocked the door to the root cellar. My friend and I ducked that doorway, ducked a doorway that once I hadn't had to, and we went down into its belly.

I remember you.

I was not down there long. The impression that the house was somewhere between awake and asleep was something my brother and I would discuss later at that place between awareness and drifting, at least until we went into the root cellar.

The house woke up.

It could simply be that my mind takes things to a dark place, but it recognized me. It had not forgotten me any more than I'd forgotten it, and at that moment, the only thing in the world I wanted to do was leave. I thanked the occupants and left immediately.

It's weird. I once lived in that house, haunted by whatever was in there, however many there were; it was always like being crammed into an overcrowded room, even though there was so much space. It was probably one of the biggest houses I've ever lived in.

I couldn't wrap my head around it, how something so big could close in on you so much and make you feel so constricted, so claustrophobic.

At first glance, it was a nice enough place to live. The single-family historic home looked pretty, and its 9,583 square foot lot (including the backyard) meant plenty of space for a family to grow, but once inside, the pervasive presence of the house itself made it feel smaller.

How we lasted there two years, living in layers of denial, escapes me. I see my children, and I know that if we lived in a house like this, I'd be looking for a new place. I'd pay the fines or penalties for early termination of a lease. I'd suffer an extra month's rent. I'd do anything to prevent something like what I went through from happening again.

I intended to check in with that family again and return the following year to find out they had moved. I found the house empty and sleeping again, blinds drawn up so that the freshly painted interior was visible from the outside. There was new carpet on the floors, and the front and backyard looked immaculate. The house sat like a sleeping demon on the Grand Circle, waiting for new residents like a carnivorous plant patiently waiting for its next meal.

The front and back doors had padlocks around the doorknobs, which real estate companies use to stow keys so their agents can give eager families a tour of the property.

Who will live there next? It could be you.

Excited families tour, and just like test driving a new car, they explore the living room, the sizable den, and the well-lit kitchen from those six-foot-high windows staring down from above.

Looking at the empty house from the outside, I realized then that it wasn't ever a predator waiting from the brush to strike; it was the predator and the brush, a monster camouflaged under the guise of a single-family home. By the time you realized it was a trap, it was because you were already in it.

I didn't approach it or attempt to get near it. I was alone, and even though I was now twenty-two, I was not—am not —ashamed to admit that I was afraid of that house. It wasn't just the rotting odors or the manifestation of apparitions; it wasn't the footsteps or the sense of dread. It was the weight I felt when even near it. I know that a lot of the weight is just the memory I carried with me, coupled with the things that happened, the fighting between Mom and Dad, the constant tension, and that echo was just as heavy as the oppressive air that surrounded that old place.

I did walk the old neighborhood, half-concerned that my car wouldn't be there when I got back. I visited old spots I favored as a child, hopeful of reclaiming some of the happiness I'd experienced there in my youth and desperate not to at the same time.

The doghouse that sat on the way to my old bus stop was still there, the chain still attached to it, but in a rusted pile at its entry, an ancient sun-bleached and cracked plastic bowl to the side.

I did this for about half an hour before I ended up at the front door of my old friend Robert's house. For no particular reason, I decided to knock. I had no idea if he still lived there, but when he answered the door, saying I was shocked would be an understatement. I was eight when I met him; he was about six or eight years old when I moved out. At that moment, I was twenty-two staring at a twenty-year-old Robert standing before me.

He didn't even pause to reveal excitement. He recognized me immediately and gave me a handshake and a hug. He asked how and what I was doing, and whether I was moving back to the old neighborhood.

We caught up for a good hour, with me vehemently denying any notion of moving back and even explaining why. It was one of the better encounters I had while in that old neighborhood, visiting the echoes of something I couldn't reclaim but could not escape.

I politely declined to come inside, explaining that I had to get home, but promised I would visit again sometime.

After getting into my car, I just sat in the driveway of that old house. I couldn't understand my draw to the damned place, a body all its own, a heart and stomach beneath it, always hungry, always waiting.

I realized with a terrible reflection of honesty that if I could afford it, I would have rented or purchased it. I couldn't even tell you why I'd ever return to such a place, but the thought was brief enough to compartmentalize the idea out of my head and go home.

I didn't discuss this with anyone, my return, again, to that old place, though I pondered why I felt the impulse to keep returning.

Part of me wished someone would flatten that place to the ground, fill its root cellar with concrete, and leave it an empty lot, and part of me hoped that I would have a chance to study it some day and find out what exactly it was that made that place such a hateful, horrible place, and why.

I was engaged to my best friend and hoping to do something with my life that Mom and Dad could not. Maybe start a family and be the father mine couldn't be. My wedding was on the horizon, and I wanted to put these sorrows away. Deal with them later. Swallow the pain. Bury it down and forget it. Just like I always had before.

NOVEMBER 22, 2002

I married my best friend in February of 2002. I was neither the husband I hoped to be, nor did I achieve fatherhood in a marriage that lasted barely nine months. My wife and I were separated at the time, and I could not help but see the correlation between my past and present.

In no uncertain terms, I loved this woman so deeply and dearly I could not comprehend why I resented her. It wasn't a matter of chance because she was the same person I'd known since I was eighteen, the same friend with whom I'd shared hopes and dreams, heartache, and fear. She'd even seen me weep at the passing of my Grandma Denney only a year before.

I understood Mom and Dad better; I understood marriage wasn't equivalent to love and happiness in

Hope Spring's Eternal. Whatever dosh idealistic people say.

What I learned instead was that sometimes the things that attract us to other people are echoes of something we wanted, missed, or wished we could have had. We create these ideas of who the person is and cling to them. Then, when they're not this idealized fiction we've created, we hurt. We hurt, we get angry, bitter, and resentful, and ultimately, we make one another miserable.

I was not who she wanted me to be, and she was nowhere near who I desired her to be, but I loved her all the same. I hated that we could not get along, no matter how hard we tried. Everything I did frustrated and annoyed her; everything she did frustrated and annoyed me.

I understood Mom's secret crying on the back porch steps of my childhood. I understood that she loved Dad, and Dad loved her, and that love wasn't enough.

They were different people with different goals, just like me and my first wife.

We were so young. She was nineteen, and I was twenty-two. She wasn't finished with the exploration of her youth. She still desired experimentation and adventure, and domestication prevented her from doing that. So, we went our separate ways.

So, I was on my own again and left with my thoughts to ponder. With my ex-wife to be moved out, I needed a roommate and found that in one of my friends. The year was spent with me burying any of the pain that bothered me, distracting myself in the company of my friends, and working as much as I could.

Without realizing it, I did something eleven years prior I'd condemned my dad for, and I began dating.

I ended up dating a sweet enough nineteen-year-old girl and quickly discovered she was not the answer to my pain. Still, we ended up together about a year before things began falling apart after she insisted a year was enough time for me to know whether to marry her. She gave me an ultimatum of marriage, and I broke up with her shortly after. Then I broke up with her again, and again for an additional couple of months, because she kept refusing my break ups.

Despite how badly things went between us as a couple, we did end up making a good friendship out of the broken pieces and still get along today. Although conversations are rare, there is no bitterness between us.

Then, I made things worse for myself. What I needed to do was be single, mourn my failed marriage, get mentally and emotionally healthy, talk to someone about the shit I'd gone through as a kid, and clean out my proverbial baggage.

What I did instead was become a serial monogamist. I didn't bother dating; I just jumped into relationships until they burned out, and they either broke up with me or I broke up with them, whoever they were.

By 2006, I was in a dysfunctional relationship with the daughter of a world-renowned painter. I was a twice-published author by this time, had three book signings, and worked with my friends to bolster my writing career. The books I wrote were based around ongoing nightmares I'd had since I was a child, some of which included the house, some of which alluded to the house, and some of which were inspired by dark places my mind goes to when I witness things that scare me.

I never made it further than being a local author. Book signings always sold out, and by 2007, an intern working for a rather famous movie producer solicited me for a copy of my book, promotional material, and all the things that could potentially drive value if my book were turned into a movie.

I sincerely thought I'd made the big time. Things were proceeding as I'd never experienced in my life, and it made the dysfunction in my relationship tolerable. I had a team of people I trusted, my closest friends, helping me push this forward. Honest to God's truth, we almost made it.

We almost made it.

Then, the project was shelved. My girlfriend and I broke up. I stopped writing, stopped trying, and did something I hadn't done in a long time. I went back to the damned house on West Grand.

This time, though, I went with my mom. She didn't ask why I wanted to go and didn't pretend to understand why I wanted to go, but after lunch, we began talking about the house, my exes, and why I kept finding myself in bad relationships.

Mom parked where Dad used to park his car, in the parking area next to the garage. The gate was still there, the house empty, the yard bearing fruit from the orange tree and the pomegranate bush.

I went into the yard and then into the garage. I don't know why. I don't know what I expected, but the garage was empty. It was empty in the same way the house was silent the night my dad and sister went out to pick up some junk food and bring it home; when I was alone for only a short time (which felt like an eternity)—*that* silence.

Except this wasn't exactly that silence. This was something else, something new. It was more like dead silence, like being in the company of a corpse. No presence. No weight. Nothing.

The garage was empty, but Dad's bumper stickers were at the far end of the wall. I hurried to them. They were faded, brittle, not peeling off the wall, cracked in places where fissures had formed, cracked open over quarter-inch breaks.

Had anyone at all lived here since the last family? Had anyone taken the time to prevent this place from falling into disrepair? It didn't seem like it. Like Dad, the garage was cracked, not necessarily breaking apart, but cracked and dead.

I said that, at that moment. *Cracked and dead, like my father.*

When I left the garage, got back into the car with my mom, and buckled in, she asked if I'd seen anything. I told her about the disrepair and that the wall in the garage had a large crack in it, splitting Dad's bumper stickers apart. I'd mentioned that I'd said it was cracked and dead like my father, and she laughed and declared I was morbid and a bit overdramatic.

Still, she was noticeably happier as we pulled away and put the house in her rearview mirror. The house was still there, but if the house was still there if the entities that inhabited it were still there, I couldn't tell. Maybe they were gone. Perhaps they were gone because there were no more families left to consume, and they'd moved on to terrorize some other family somewhere else.

I want to think that was it. I'd like to believe that the House on West Grand and all its terrible memories were dead, gone, and away.

I want to tell you as much, but I'd be lying.

THE PRD

Until this point, I'd been wrestling with whether or not to confess that my experience on October 27, 2001, with my friend led to us founding—alongside two others who'd had a strange experience that same day—a little paranormal investigation team we called the PRD (paranormal research and development).

Around the time I was telling you about the woman behind the door, I also told you that there are no experts in the afterlife, no one who knows anything more than anyone else. There are only the people who want to understand what's happening and the people who pretend to know what's happening.

We four, that October 27, 2001, at 7:25 PM, recognized that all the television shows and all the hype we read in books were, by comparison, relatively tame.

Suppose none of it was based on any facts whatsoever. That made it pseudoscience at best.

We learned a lot in the following days, weeks, and months about the unknown. We realized charlatanism had put an irremovable stain on paranormal investigation. The field was barely limping along, except as entertainment on television.

The shows themselves were wildly popular. All of us had watched those reality shows where they jump at every shadow and ask, "What was that? Did you hear that?" are true entertainment. It's a spectacle of the spectacular.

But I must say, they don't remotely capture the horror of the real experience.

I've been to the Queen Mary, the Whaley House, and the Winchester House. I've been to Virginia City on guided tours I can't name in writing because I haven't experienced anything in them. I've seen no manifestations nor felt a presence in any of them. There were no disembodied voices or evidence to convince me that orbs are more than backscatter.

The shows we watch are spooky fun that always ends up inconclusive, with the various ghost-hunting teams sharing personal experiences and discussing what they believe went on. Roll credits. Next show.

I'm the furthest thing from a skeptic. I believe so much I must find logical conclusions to the unexplained. There aren't always answers. The purpose of the PRD in its inception was to help discover causes for my and the other group member's prior inexplicable experiences.

Not surprisingly, the only thing we uncovered were more questions and absolutely no answers.

We researched properties in Corona, notorious for hauntings. Some were harrowing to the near equivalence of the House on West Grand. I felt some twisting sense of vindication during those visits that I had others with me to also witness the frightening phenomena.

We investigated every alleged haunting and urban legend. We dug through the haunted section of our local library, and interviewed any consenting paranormal witness we could locate. Of the hundreds of haunted sites we investigated, there were maybe four places I discovered to be legitimate. Two of those four places I would proclaim to be sinister and unsettling.

I didn't include any of these physical locations because curious people visit, perpetuate urban legends, or show up on the doorsteps of individuals or families who may not want random ghost hunters popping by unannounced. There are plenty of books which contain the addresses of commercial locations that happily offer overnight stays or guided tours for people curious to learn more about the paranormal.

The PRD ran operations in Corona from 2001 to 2008. I reopened its operation in Fresno, California. In the five years that I lived in Fresno, I took a lot of phone calls, and I recorded complaints about alleged poltergeists and questions about *shadow people* and sleep paralysis. I spent a lot of time studying and researching information on possible causes, learning the phenomena of pareidolia and apophenia and the likeliest probabilities for sleep paralysis.

I didn't see a single haunting, and for the places I worked that were reputed to be haunted, if they were at all, I never experienced such a thing.

In all the time I've investigated, researched, and studied, the only conclusion I've drawn is that no living person knows anything about the paranormal. There are no experts. Expertise requires study and experimentation, and those experiments require repeatable results. Paranormal investigation is a maddening pseudoscience whose following must create answers to fill in the gaps because there are none.

It's a bleak study, yet I am still not a cynic.

The Woman Behind the Door was not pareidolia, nightmare, or imagination. The Bloody Mary a troubled little girl's bad dream. The footsteps and the shaking blinds, the interactions with our dog Stormy—these things happened, and there is no reasonable, rational, or logical explanation. That house gave us proof without leaving evidence. After all, it's not what you know; it's what you can prove.

OCTOBER 2008

It was October of 2008, and I was three months from leaving Corona and moving to Fresno when I returned to West Grand. The house had been fully renovated, the backyard removed and replaced, the trees gone, and the pomegranate bush was gone. They tore down the garage to make extra space.

At the time, I was writing articles about the PRD's exploits on a now long-defunct paranormal website. One of those articles (that disappeared from the website) was about the house, and someone responded to the article. Some lady I've never met who called herself Margie May said she knew the owners.

We exchanged emails, and she explained to me the new owners moved in October of 2008, and they almost immediately noticed something was wrong with the house. They'd contacted her and asked her to perform a cleansing on the house, which she agreed to do. According to her, the house was no longer haunted and evil. Margie May said the nightmare was over for everyone, past and present.

I didn't believe her because I knew enough to know there were no shortcuts or easy answers by then. I didn't believe burning armpit-scented herbs and telling something to get out was effective. I consider it to be a tactic used by people who make up their own rules.

In Margie's defense, her beliefs and spiritualism *stemmed* from the American Spiritualism movement, which spanned the 1850s through the 1920s. Embers of these old practices still exist in splinter groups just about everywhere. Anyone who does a little digging can learn more about it.

So, Margie May decided the house was free of evil. I didn't bother to contact the owners because there was no sense in frightening them—considering they were believers—and creating any hysteria, especially on the off chance that the house was clear and free of entities.

So, not feeling any better about it, I took one last drive through the old neighborhood. I was moving soon, and it was time to say my goodbyes.

My, how the house had changed. It wasn't just a nice-looking house; it was beautiful how they dressed it up and made it their own. They'd even transformed the root cellar into an additional bedroom.

I can't tell you how it made my skin crawl to see that the heart and belly of that old house had been turned into a place where people slept.

I didn't spend too much time around the house. It wasn't mine anymore. I didn't want to be a stranger lurking in a neighborhood.

I did a lot of thinking while I was there and took a stroll through the old backways of the neighborhood, the poorly kept single-car streets that allowed the people living on that grid access to and from their homes. The air smelled like I remembered that hopeful October when I was convinced that things would be fine for Mom and Dad. It brought reflection, memories, and the thought that the house reminded me of a tomb. No, not a tomb. Something else. There's an old name for places like that.

Whited Sepulcher. Things that are beautiful on the outside, trimmed in splendor and decoration, but are a place of the dead, where the body breaks down and rots.

When I look back at the house in those days, I couldn't think of a better description for a more deserving property, except perhaps an ossuary. An ossuary is a container or place where the bones of the dead are kept.

To the best of my knowledge, being that there have never been headlines to the contrary, the house on West Grand Boulevard had neither kept the bones of the dead in any room nor under any floorboards, and as dramatic as it could have been, ala poltergeist movies, the house was not built over any burial grounds.

Yet, that property kept old memories like the bones of the dead, eating them up in its walls and spilling them out for all to bear witness; it was a handsome house that would later be decorated in such splendor as any whited sepulcher, but inside of that house, not the rooms or the root cellar, but the very core of that house itself was unclean things that tormented our family.

I reminisced as I walked those back streets. I was still a child, only a month into living at the house when a stranger had entered our property. Stormy was usually hostile to strangers because he was a good boy and protector of our family.

Still, he was indifferent when this stranger, who later turned out to be our neighbor, entered our yard where my dad and I were playing. He introduced himself to Dad and me and asked if we'd always had the dog.

Dad assured him that we had, and the guy was relieved. He explained that the former neighbors had a dog that looked very much like Stormy, named Sparky—a name I have *always* felt was a lazy name for a dog—that had died on the property.

The hairs on the man's arms were standing on end. He'd confessed as much that it scared him when he'd seen Stormy because, to the best of his knowledge, that dog had died, and he'd never actually seen our dog. He had started to mention the house's previous occupants, looked at me, and thought better of it. Afterward, he thanked us for our time and left the property.

I want to believe he was about to tell us confidently about the complaints the previous renters made to him about the bad things in that house and decided not to because I was there. It would make for much more dramatic storytelling, and I suppose if this weren't a true story, that's where I'd take it, but he didn't.

The man was unnerved, but I don't (and will never) know if he had anything to say about the house. Back then, I'd already had my unwelcome meeting with the woman behind the door, but I wasn't about to bring it up—especially not to the stranger—because I wasn't about to share something like that with anyone, not my family.

There were more than a few times that passersby would ask if our dog's name was Sparky and more than a few times, older kids in the neighborhood would *argue* that our dog was Sparky, not Stormy.

The memories made me miss Stormy.

In 2008, I'd owned a few dogs to follow, all fiercely loyal, funny animals with unique personalities, quirks, and temperaments. However, to date, none of them was anything like Stormy, and that's not nostalgia talking. Stormy was precisely who my family needed when they needed him.

After I stopped speaking to Dad, before we reunited, Dad had given Stormy to a neighbor when he moved overseas. I never saw that good dog again, and between strolling my old haunts, or more to the point, this old place that haunted me, and the scent of memories in the air, I found myself missing many things.

It was close to evening, and I had one last stop to make before I left.

Robert was happy to see me, as delighted as he ever was any time I encountered him by happenstance outside of the neighborhood, whether he happened to be shopping when I was out getting groceries or just passing at a traffic light.

We caught up again, this man in his mid-twenties now, and by the time we said our goodbyes, it was dark out. I explained that I was moving soon and wanted an opportunity to convey a proper goodbye.

We stood at his porch, adjacent to an old and rusting swing set in a terrible state of disrepair, a swing set I'd fixed for him when I was nine.

The echoes of his young voice still make me smile because when I fixed it when I was nine, he'd called me a hero. To that memory, I had never been called a hero, and I couldn't understand how heroic fixing something as trivial as a swing set could be.

Still, standing across from Robert, all grown up, that memory cemented itself in my mind.

There's so much satisfaction in seeing the kids we knew when we were young grow into fine young adults. I didn't know Robert well anymore, but I could tell by seeing and talking to him that he had a good head on his shoulders, and something inside me said he would do well for himself.

I told him that this was probably it for me, the last visit to the neighborhood, and that I was due to move to the central valley in a couple of months.

I suppose the moment was a little maudlin, but it was a lesson I'd learned that people go—they always go—but leaving wasn't always a bad thing. I didn't bother to express as much because there was no sense in saying anything he'd eventually learn.

I don't know if the man ever thinks of me or if he still remembers me; I don't know if I had any lasting effect on his life, but it wouldn't matter if I did.

I remember Robert.

NEW YEAR'S 2008:
CLOVIS, CALIFORNIA

It was a new year, a new city, and a new life for me.
My fiancée's daughter adopted me as her daddy, and
my fiancée had my firstborn daughter just a few months
away from coming into the world.

One day, for no good reason at all, I decided to
check my PRD email. I had a flagged email from Margie
May. I hadn't checked this email account in some time,
and the date was in October 2008. It was an urgent
email, written in all caps, and when I opened it, I could
promise that I nearly vomited.

*I need your phone number! Why is the house more active in
October? What is in there? How Many? The owners are scared.*

They have inexplicably gotten sick! Strange things are going on. They are asking for help. Please email me back!

I replied, but never heard back. To my knowledge, the house's owners recovered, but they later transferred ownership to a relative.

I never attempted to contact the new owners and won't. Whatever is or isn't happening, I would like to believe it finally stopped. I don't know what happened to Margie May. She was already older when I started corresponding with her initially, and if she's still out there, she's not up to trading emails.

I won't give up the address for the same reason I wouldn't any other site I've ever investigated. The owners deserve peace of mind; they can't have that if anyone starts knocking on their door.

Besides, if there were still something, it wouldn't be something that anyone with a Gauss meter and a burning stick of sage could throw out.

That house is four-hundred-thirty-five miles away from where I live now. It has haunted me for thirty-three years of my life, occupying space in my head and lending generous nightmares for just as long a time.

When I began writing this at forty-two, I did so with the same fear as that poor eight-year-old kid whose dad made the nightly checks beneath the bed. I feel silly writing that in my mid-life. I feel foolish admitting I am still shaken by something that happened so long ago.

It astounds me the things I've shared and the things I can't share that belong to people who wouldn't want to be named in this story. I understand why they would choose not to share their own stories. You tell someone something like this, and you're off to get a psych eval.

Almost half of the US population believes in an afterlife, and only slightly less in the UK. Chances are that most people have a haunting to talk about, but no one wants to volunteer their stories because nobody takes them seriously.

There are case studies in phasmophobia and an entire syndrome named after haunted people (and recognizing the patterns in these people). Ghost stories around the campfire, during sleepovers, or in internet forums are fun because they set a tone and a mood. By morning, it was all just a story, taken as make-believe. It's alright. Everything is okay.

They're just stories.

Until they're not.

After reading Margie May's email, I checked the old paranormal website, logged in, and read my article about the house on West Grand. I had a new message, but the writer mentioned me by my full name, and I'd never used my name on the website. The message on my article had been posted roughly around the same time I'd gotten my letter from Margie May in October 2008.

I didn't save it, though I wish I had both the email and that message saved; had I known or had the foresight that I would write about this one day, I suppose I'd have done just that.

The anonymous message asked if I was Michael Oka and if I knew any more about the house than I'd shared.

I needed to keep on top of my emails more often, but the truth was I was going to be a daddy, and nothing was more on my mind than the thought of meeting my new baby girl when it was time to do that.

Like so many bad decisions I'd made, this relationship wouldn't last.

A lifetime of stewing over the discontent of a broken family has led me through some very unhealthy relationships. I wasn't guiltless in a long line of failed relationships. I rushed headlong into situations with women I barely knew, and then we'd resent one another for not being the people we hoped for in each other. When one relationship ended, I'd date for too short a time, end up in a relationship, and it would deteriorate. This continued until I met the mother of my children.

Now, I was living with her in Clovis, California. We barely knew one another; she was pregnant, and we were engaged.

I knew this was an enormous risk. I understood the odds were not in my favor and the way we fought as the months continued into our first apartment and onward. When my daughter was born, my whole worldview changed. It should have changed a lot more. Being a man meant working relentlessly, earning a living, and supporting my family. I labored long hours, subcontracted to a central valley military base through a major aerospace company, in counter surveillance, entry control, and training military personnel in small arms.

I woke up at 3:45 AM, left for work by 4:00 AM, clocked in at 5:00 AM, and clocked out at 5:00 PM. When I got home, I ate dinner, spent an hour or two with my family, went to bed, and repeated the process five days a week.

I never complained about my hours, and I threw myself into my job because I thought that was what a man was supposed to do and supposed to be. Meanwhile, I saw less of my family, and even after my wife gave birth to my firstborn, I worked.

I was exhausted all the time, but I pushed through it. The hours shortened my already short fuse. I fought more with my wife, and numerous times, one of us would threaten to leave.

I did this for ten months, missing out on so many things. I thought a husband and father's sole purpose was only to provide. It never seemed enough for all the money I was making. We were always broke after paying the bills, but I kept working.

When my contract ended, I took up work in security and sometimes worked seven days a week, sleeping during the day to be up in time for dinner and off to work late hours.

The owner of the security company and I became close friends. Still, when I noticed things started to spiral out of control and he was beginning to do things well out of bounds, I sought other employment and thanked him for the opportunities he'd provided.

Then, just like that, I was a bouncer again. I was doing the same work I'd done when I first met my second wife. The pay was terrible, but I worked any hours the club owner needed, and before a year, I'd become close friends with the owner.

The man was generous. He gave me a raise when I told him I needed to make more money. When I was short on cash, the man paid my bills. He cared for my family and me, so I stayed with his club for five years.

In 2014, my wife found a job listing for a mountain security job. We thought it was relatively close to us, but the job was at a top-rated ski resort with a trendy corporation.

I've been in security since I was twenty, almost every kind of security. I'd done foot patrols, walking apartment complexes from dusk until dawn. I'd taken vehicle patrols. I accepted work in event security and short run-in close protection (colloquially known as *bodyguards*. I'd been in fugitive recovery, and lastly, I had been a well-accomplished bouncer for some prominent strip clubs.

The jump to mountain security would be a culture shock for me, but I'd still have a month remaining at the club.

Then I found out that the mountain for which I would fall in love was four hours from where I lived, four hours from my wife and children; it was two-hundred-twenty-seven miles from home. I would have to live there in employee housing. I accepted the job. It paid well, and my experience ensured I would get an excellent wage.

In October of 2014, without even realizing it, as my wife dropped me off on the mountain, I became John Oka.

The mountain was an adventure. It was exciting and unforgettable; it was like nothing I'd ever done, and for their culture, I was no one that mountain had ever experienced. I felt appreciated, and my experience was respected. I was lauded as the first consistent enforcer they had ever seen, and my reputation grew through the mountain and the company.

When I was hired, the hiring manager (a good friend of mine now) told me in the past, security had been inconsistent. It had been too wishy-washy and unpredictable, and many employee housing employees had become out of control. He told me he needed a soldier for the field, so I changed the mountain and the culture.

I helped write the security manual for the security department, trained all incoming officers, and taught the officers staging points and how we could regain control of the mountain for the security office and the corporation. Then, within one month, the mountain was under control. It all came down to a matter of maintaining that control benevolently.

Meanwhile, I learned how to utilize the tools the mountain had given me to enforce policy and protect good employees put into compromising positions by staff.

Unfortunately, I'd gained a nickname that spread up to the president of the mountain. More and more, I became known as *the hammer*.

When you're a hammer, everything else is just a nail.

However, at the time, it had been stressed to me that a hammer was what the mountain needed. I was thirty-four, idealistic, and embraced my role.

Food shipments came to me once a month. I saw my wife and kids once a month. I lost a lot of weight both practicing and teaching martial arts.

I received service awards and changed how safety was practiced on the mountain. I also tracked every emergency light on the mountain, and I streamlined a process, cutting the time it to test from six to eight hours to three- or four-hours so that an officer could perform the function even on a busy day.

The map is still used to this day.

At the end of the season, nine months after I started, I transferred to a year-round mountain in Truckee, California. Same corporation, different mountain. I worked there for a year, and the corporation started emailing me, asking what kind of officer my prior mountain needed and how to maintain employee retention for the coming season. I shared my opinions, and these practices were implemented.

It was 2015, finally, I'd gotten what I needed: my family.

We moved to Dayton, Nevada. It was a quiet, middle-of-nowhere town about twenty minutes from Carson City. Once again, I worked graveyard shifts, slept days, and earned.

By March 2016, the Mountain Operations director emailed me, telling me they had trouble retaining and training officers, and asked me to return to the mountain. One year to the day I left, I returned to the mountain where it all began.

In 2017, I caught my wife expressing that she was unhappy and wanted a divorce. The marriage wasn't working. She desired something else she wasn't sure what, but it wasn't being somebody's wife.

She explained that all her life, she had always been the daughter in service to her mother, the girlfriend, the mother, and the wife. Yet, she had never had a life of her own.

So, this was what it was like to be John Oka. You got this for adventure, travel, and throwing yourself into work. It wasn't until I caught her with a mutual friend and coworker that I understood the things she said prior were a lie.

When I met her, I was a high-earning bouncer making so much money I only really had to work a few days a week. She'd just come out of a relationship, and her ex had stopped sharing his substantial earnings. The man I caught her with had a lot of money saved up, and though he didn't make more than me, he was younger than me, had more money than I did, and represented an opportunity that I did not. This had been going on for a while.

Just like that, we split up. My poor children.

I failed them so completely. I couldn't hold a family together, and the only reason I'd stayed married to a woman who hated me, who I wasn't particularly fond of, was all for nothing. Worst of all, she had taken work at the mountain, so even the mountain I loved had become a hostile working environment.

In February of 2018, I was hospitalized. What had been going on for months, but somehow, I didn't feel it;

I'd developed a half-dollar-sized hole in my duodenum.

I'd originally gone to the doctor thinking I had the flu. When the doctor presented me with having tested positive for influenza as good news, I wasn't prepared for what came next.

I had only seven units of blood in my body. I was bleeding to death internally. How fortunate, they said, that I had come in. Another day or two, and I would have gone to sleep and died. So, they admitted me. That night, while I was attempting to make it to the restroom, I collapsed and hit my head on the hospital room floor. I woke up an hour later, and I was weak.

Every bone ached, and I could barely lift a hand off the floor. I stared at the side of my hospital bed, the nurse's call button. I contemplated *not* pushing that button. How easy would it be just to let go? For all the aching in my body, it didn't hurt. Dying wasn't painful. If I just went to sleep, that would be it. I stared at the call button and took a shallow breath. I closed my eyes.

Then, there was only darkness. *No.*

I remember opening my eyes. I had three kids who needed me. Everything that led to this point was a struggle in trying to get my estranged wife even to bother coming home to watch the kids so I could go to my shift at work. She said our eldest could watch the younger two while I was at work. I'd found myself calling into work late almost daily while looking for a sitter. Frequently. When I couldn't find a sitter, I had to call in.

I'd never been late once in all my time with the company. I had zero write-ups. I had never called off. All of that was unwound, and it didn't matter. Yet, if I died,

I'd be calling out of life, leaving my children to a future without me as a counterbalance.

My leg was stiff and heavy, sore, and just lifting it off the hospital floor left me panting for breath, but my big toe found the call button. Then darkness again.

Darkness. Light. Unconscious. Conscious. Nurses lifted me off the hospital room floor. I was only thirty-eight. I had to outlive my father's years. I was only thirty-seven. John had made it to forty-one.

I could not do this to my kids.

They would lift me onto the bed, but I wouldn't have it. I'd pissed my pants. They're saying it's okay, but I was not having it. I had to use the restroom. A nurse escorted me to the bathroom, where I vomited blood on the way there. I had to use the toilet. The nurse, some poor kid maybe in his late twenties, was standing there. I told him to get the hell out, and *man*, I was aggressive. He says it's okay, and I told him to get the fuck out, or I'll make him.

I would find out later that the amount of blood I'd sustained had me functioning out of some primal part of my brain responsible for aggression.

I remember I was *so* thirsty, but they'd said I could neither eat nor drink anything until they'd tended to my bleeding ulcer. So, I pulled my pants up and demanded the nurse put me in the shower. The shower was just a tiled step that doubled as a seat, but he said no, that it was fine. I told him I wouldn't leave without a shower. So, he put me in the shower as two additional nurses stood by. When the water came on, it soaked my shirt, pants, and underclothes. I stripped down while sneaking small gulps of water from the shower head.

Then I forget. I forget everything until I wake up in a bed, in a hospital gown. The doctor was there, telling me he hadn't realized how much blood I was losing, but I was down to five units. He asked me if I knew my blood type, but I uttered a long stream of gibberish when I tried to tell him. I couldn't talk. At all. I couldn't formulate a sentence. I could think about it and knew what I wanted to say, but it came out in sounds that weren't words.

The doctor told me to try not to talk. I needed a blood transfusion. I was losing too much blood too fast, and there needed to be an emergency blood transfusion. I had to sign the paperwork, which I did by making an X on all the parts I was supposed to sign because I couldn't write my name for my life—literally, for my life.

Then, I don't remember. It's just darkness. By the time I woke up, there were bags of blood, and I'd finally earned the nickname "Nosferoka" that my cohorts had given me on the mountain. I was pale, had enormous canines, and ate my steaks cooked blue (if you've never had a blue steak, that is where all the flavor is). *Now*, I was taking blood into my body. Blood that wasn't mine.

I laughed. Within a half hour, I could speak again and think clearly, and I felt much better, but it wasn't over yet. Memory fails me. Then I'm in the operating room, there's a mask over my face, and the anesthesiologist is asking me questions. Then it's all just darkness again. Absolute darkness, and it's beautiful. When I wake up in recovery, the procedure's been a success.

I'm alive, and I'm so thankful for it. All the despair I'd felt was gone—all the aggression, gone. I would live to father my children.

The doctor explained that because I'd spent so much time at altitude, I had, on average, sixteen units of blood in my body. After my transfusion, I had nine, and it would be a while before I completely recovered. He wanted me to take a few weeks off work, and I told him I couldn't. The doctor explained that I couldn't walk long distances or drive if I returned to work. I agreed and would sit as a passenger during vehicle patrols.

They took me back to my hospital room, and I slept. A co-worker and good friend were at my bedside when I woke up. He just wanted to ensure I was alive and share it with our other friends back on the mountain. He was there, and then he was gone. I fell asleep. Cousins came and went, seeing I was sleeping. When I woke up again, Mom sat by my bedside with a get-well balloon.

God, I love my mom. I love my cousins. One of my cousins used her miles to get my mom on a plane flight out, and Mom stayed long enough to see me back on my feet. She was gone, then, and I was back to the mountain. In March of 2018, I was released as a seasonal officer. I had become unreliable. The department manager insisted he couldn't be sure I'd be late for work. I was devastated. I'd given four years of my life and only a year left before I got my five-year pin, but he was right. So long as I had kids, there was no decision to be made.

So, I was laid off as a seasonal employee. I didn't panic, I didn't worry. I applied for unemployment and immediately began looking for work. I knew who to call. I called the man who'd initially brought me to the mountain. He now worked for a prominent and world-famous brand-name hotel and casino at Stateline Nevada. I contacted him and asked if they had positions open, and once again, he had a job for me, just as he had in 2014.

I worked a shift that worked with my children's schedule so that I could work and be a father.

When they first came into my life, I promised myself I would be a better father to them than my dad was to me, but that took more time than it should have. Like my dad, I threw myself into my work and the sudden drive to travel.

It wasn't until my last wife left, and I nearly died that I finally broke the cycle my father left in his wake. I went from being a father to being a daddy, from being a drill instructor to being as much fun as I was dad. Equal parts a toy as much as I was not just daddy, not just dad, but an actual father to my children.

I'm so proud of my children. They expressed their sorrow to me, their misery in the divorce, and I have had to, on more than one occasion, explain that Mom and Dad love them all very much. That the divorce was because neither of us could get along. I would do anything to ensure they had the best childhood possible. I would never live away from home again; I would never work hundreds of miles from them.

Words are cheap. So, I proved it, and I became someone my father never managed. In doing this, I could forgive my father—really forgive him—for not being present, even for the years I'd driven him away.

I spent three years working at the hotel and casino, rocking hard to good music, and once again breaking records in how security was run. Through ups and downs, the experience was probably the best I'd had yet. I worked harder than ever, pushing myself to beat my records and drive morale and hard work.

During my early days employed with that company, I showed my divorce. It was made official. We would have equal custody of the children in every way. In all that time, two weeks on, two weeks off, I'd dated, but I rushed into nothing. I allowed myself time to heal, even when it was painful and lonely. I made do.

I dated on and off for a year, and there were a couple of times I thought things might go somewhere with a woman. Still, I recognized in myself that I was emotionally unavailable and would not subject myself or anyone else to a relationship with someone whose wounds were still as fresh as mine.

In 2019, I made friends with a coworker. She and I traded books and spoke over lunch breaks at work. We hung out outside work, meeting for lunch and discussing whatever struck our fancy. We eventually did start dating, and even then, we both felt that there was nothing worth rushing. It was six months before she met my children. It was a slow introduction. My eldest daughter, who adopted me, was eighteen. My two younger kids were nine and six.

In 2020, everything changed.

A new virus was out and about, and no one knew what it was or how to handle it. My girlfriend and I discussed our living arrangements. We concluded that it might be easier to move in together, consolidate our resources, and run a household, but it wouldn't be a pandemic that forced our hand. We opted to wait.

This is the first truly healthy relationship I'd ever been in, and I'll be honest. I didn't feel I deserved it. We talked things out. When we argued, we didn't scream or call one another names. We found resolutions and helped one another grow in our relationship. She shared everything with me, and I shared everything with her. Our relationship survived the pandemic.

Just before the summer of 2020, Mom moved to Carson City, Nevada. Mom and I were strained at first. I gave her my room and slept in the living room. Before winter 2020, Mom got her own place, and I moved into a new apartment.

Then, just like that, it was announced that it was safe to return to work. I returned to the hotel and casino while my girlfriend worked at a bank. Day in and day out, I worked under a new regime. I worked directly for the man who made northern Nevada a possibility for me, and I was allowed the room for growth to teach and train. They still use the training videos I created just before I left in 2021.

In July of 2022, my girlfriend and I married. Before we did, I asked all three of my children for permission to marry again. They all permitted me, provided I wasn't trying to replace their mom in their lives. My girlfriend would speak to them later and tell them she had no desire to replace anyone. Her goal was to be their advocate, friend, and ally; no matter what, she would always be there for them.

So, we married.

I can't tell you the relief I feel, having met someone, and allowed myself the room and the space to let that relationship grow organically. I'd never worked through an argument before, but I had no anger or rage left. I'd never known what a healthy relationship was, but she and I worked through things together. I'd gotten past waiting for the other shoe to drop and accepted that it was all right for me to be happy.

My entire life, I'd been at war. I moved often and was taught how to survive in no uncertain terms. I'd survived divorce, death, and sorrow. The war was over, and I had no idea what to do when the war was over. What do you do when it's time to lay down your arms and be happy?

I'll tell you what. You allow yourself to be happy. You let yourself to be satisfied.

I still get mad at my dad sometimes, you know? I see my kids, and I know, because of the man he had become at the end of his life, how good a grandpa he'd have been had he not squandered his life away. Then, I remind myself that we're all responsible for our choices, and nothing could have stopped my dad from meeting his end the way he did.

The nightmares haven't stopped. Occasionally, I still heard creaking joints and strained corpse flesh over old bones as hollows where eyes should have been, lifted from the carpet to meet my gaze. In these dreams, I'm not even a child. I'm an adult man, still terrified of the woman behind the door. I still sometimes wake in cold sweat, my heart pounding. The afterimages of that terror fade from their intensity as I gain my bearings.

The echoes of Mom and Dad's fights still fill dark dreams, where there is no light, no vision, no images, but only screaming in inky blackness. The sounds of my sister crying over the bloody Mary and my parents' panicked faces, knowing there was nothing they could do about it. I still see them and hear them occasionally when I sleep.

NOVEMBER 30, 2022

I was talking with my mom in late November, and the House on West Grand topic came up. My mom and I discussed it at length, and she concluded that it wasn't unusual that the old place had so much residence in my head. It was weird.

It's not weird. I told my mom. The House on West Grand was the last time I knew a complete family. It was the place where my entire life would change forever, not just because of my family but because of the horrible, awful things I experienced while I was there. The woman behind the door, my sister crying inconsolably over the Bloody Mary; Mom's experience in the living room where the house made itself known to her. It was the place where Dad's new girlfriend saw the apparition of a woman on the side of his bed. This was the last point and place where anything would be normal again.

Mom was quiet for a bit after my response, and she nodded and said I was right. I was a little boy who'd gone through hell with his family, and maybe something worse in the house that legitimately scared us all.

I've been thinking about this conversation because this creative non-fiction piece was written as a short story. It was only 11,200 words, but my feedback from the story, from Mom and a handful of people I allowed to read it, insisted this may be the best work I've ever done. A friend suggested something unexpected: that it could be a short novelization or a novella—that the story could even be a published work.

Something strange happened while I wrote it; it wasn't anything paranormal or ghostly. I'm not afraid for the first time in thirty-four years since I moved into the House on West Grand.

Since I started this piece, so much of the fear has gone to the sidelines; it's become a memory of a feeling, not the feeling itself. The weight of my familial issues in my childhood has been reconciled. The burden of the weight I've carried on my shoulders for so long has gone away.

It's the first time in thirty-four years that this house did not dominate my thoughts when I woke in the morning or before I went to bed at night, with everything that went with it.

It's the first time in thirty-four years that I feel free, something I could have done any time, except this was the right time. Now was when it mattered. I'd attempted this story three times in my life, and three times prior, it never took. It was never right. I'd never shared more than the old entities of that house whose memory stayed with me so long.

I'd only spent two years living in a haunted house, but that house haunted me for most of my life. It followed me everywhere I went, and even though I'd left Corona, it never left me. This was supposed to be the end of this story, the epiphany that settled all things.

It's not the end. Something new arose, new information—one last story to tell.

DECEMBER 17, 2022

I've mentioned Robert's name several times in the story. A neighborhood friend, someone I spent my first two years in the old neighborhood playing with. I wrote the chapter in October 2008 with the fondest memories of my farewell to the house and the neighborhood and the last time I spoke to Robert. It raised a nostalgia in me that made me miss my old friend.

I'm no fan of Social Media, but it proved helpful on December 17, 2022, when I found Robert Vargas after a brief search. I reached out, and within minutes, he responded with a funny *Oh, Snap!*

He even remembered the last time we spoke that day in October 2008.

So, we talked a bit, and I asked him if he was the anonymous commenter on the post I once posted on that paranormal website.

He was.

I explained the story I was writing about my life and the House on West Grand. He was quiet for a moment before calling me on the messenger. He'd contacted his aunt, who'd been in our old neighborhood long before he or I were born.

Robert lived in a multigenerational home; his family had long been to the Grand Circle. While his aunt hadn't been able to attest to any tales of haunting in the house itself, something he said caught my attention especially.

In his childhood, he knew that the root cellar was bad. It was something he understood as a child and that his family knew back in the 1950s. The root cellar was a bad place, though his aunt couldn't exactly explain *why*. She'd known the people who lived in the house before my family, and I had moved in. Further, she had known them for a long while. They'd lived there throughout his aunt's youth, and then one day, they just moved out, and a new family (my family) moved in.

Everyone knew to *stay out of the root cellar.*

Then he told me what his aunt told him to pass on to me. I'd mentioned in the beginning that the house was situated in such a place on West Grand that it was close to the freeway onramp. Well, in the youth of his aunt, that freeway didn't exist, but there was a pumphouse there. His aunt explained that many people in the neighborhood knew but spoke very little of it.

The White Lady of the Pump House. This didn't sound like it had anything to do with the house on West Grand until he told me something else.

It was something everyone knew about, a lady in white that manifested at the pump house and would sort of float from the pumphouse, crossing the street and taking the old back roads in our neighborhood. It would pass our house. My aunt saw it. Grandma saw it. Everyone knew about it. It had no feet, but it would sort of float past their house, down the backroads between the houses in the neighborhood, and continue toward the House on West Grand. It would stop at the house and disappear.

He explained that his aunt knew the people who lived in the house—when they moved and to where—though neither he nor she knew if they were still alive.

This house had been a thorn in the side of the old neighborhood, the seemingly unassuming, handsome, and spacious property that was less an object and more its own thing, its own self, for lack of a better word.

Whether one or many entities lived in that house, Robert alluded that the house had borne witness to bad things. The house's occupants were a mixed race couple, the husband of mixed races himself. In the 1950s, this was a particularly complicated issue, and the occupants were not spared from the bigotry of the times.

I think about that house and what it's seen. How much older it was than any of us—only forty years old (give or take) by the 1950s, and I wonder what else it had witnessed. The horrors of racial bigotry in the past, coupled with whatever things I cannot possibly know happened before or leading up to the point where my family moved in, the house saw it all. It experienced it all.

I couldn't tell you what happened from its creation in 1916 to the point where people witnessed the white lady of the pumphouse, whose path would traverse from the pumphouse, now long gone, all the way through the neighborhood and to the house where it would stop and disappear.

It begs so many questions, those famous five *W*s: who, what, when, where, and why. Yet, *no one* in the neighborhood knew who she was, could have been, or whether she was an intelligent haunting. The certainty of the tale was that *everyone* in the neighborhood had seen her at one point or another, while others saw her almost every time she took her forlorn journey, that silent sojourn from whatever it was, her point A, to its conclusion at point B.

My narrow view of the house until this conversation had been that we were the only ones this malicious house had haunted. It never dawned on me, despite seeking its unspoken—untraceable—history, that there were other stories still in reach, still alive in the voices of those I haven't seen in years or their family whom I'd maybe met once or twice at a birthday party in my youth.

I am thankful that in my youth when my parents were busy fighting or my dad's girlfriend was too foolish to keep her experience to herself, no one in Robert's family once mentioned the history of that house to me.

How badly have I wanted to contact its current owners during this story and ask them what terrible things they'd experienced or why they'd chosen to turn the root cellar into an additional bedroom on God's green earth?

When I'd first told my mom they'd turned that cellar into a room, she was shocked, asking why anyone would want to live down *there*.

There will be endless questions, but I'm satisfied with my part in this story. It's finally been told and told right. There was so much to unpack here, and while it seems that so much of it is unrelated to the house that changed my life forever, *everything* in my life was dominated by its influence and all that happened within it.

Everything, until now. Right now. When I can finally let go of the West Grand Haunting.

AFTERWORD

Mom didn't want me to push this story as creative non-fiction, and I don't blame her.

She wanted this to be a fictional story based on a true story because we can't prove our experiences. We can't ever prove the woman behind the door, the footsteps, the bloody Mary, or the strange behavior of our dog Stormy.

Like all paranormal experiences, this story is as anecdotal as the next. Mom didn't like that and felt it wasn't as honest as pushing the story as fiction based on a true story, but what is creative non-fiction, if not a souped-up story based on something that happened?

These events did happen to us. We experienced them; we had to cope with living in fear in both our physical lives—from the ever-looming threat of dissolution, dispersion, divorce, and all the bad things that come with it—and in our spiritual lives, from the steady attacks on our family's fear, from that house, that place that hated us.

Mom didn't want this story to come off as a lie, being told as a true story, but this is true. I can't prove any of the experiences I've shared in the supernatural, but these things did happen. When I asked Mom, during this conversation, whether she believed what happened to her, she replied, "I don't believe that they happened. I know they happened; I was there. I experienced it."

Since you made it this far, I'm glad to invite you to disbelieve and make this a campfire story you can tell. Omit the horrors of my childhood familial issues; ghosts can be explained far more easily than a broken family. Dumb this story down, dilute it, embellish it, or if you want, tell it to whomever you wish to as though the hauntings happened to you or someone you know.

We're no longer strangers, you and I. You've seen the darkest periods of my life, and maybe you liked or hated me; maybe you sympathized or felt pity. Perhaps you relate to me. Whether I brought out the best or the worst in you, we're no longer strangers. You may as well have been any of my neighbors in that old neighborhood watching my life unfold into what I consider to be a tragedy, and since you've witnessed now as much as that old house did and *more*, I invite you to share my story.

I've been as honest as memory serves, and to the memories serves to those who experienced it directly or had foreknowledge of the house before our arrival.

I'm glad I took my friend Ashley's advice to turn this once much shorter story into something more. I am thankful for her insight and guidance in it. My test readers for this piece insist this is the best work I've ever done, and I'm inclined to agree. Not because it's a good or bad story or because I'm playing my own trumpet. I agree for a different reason.

This story was difficult to write; I struggled through the original piece, facing things I'd buried away my whole life, whose details were dumbed down to *"I once lived in a haunted house.*" It was so much more, and I cannot stress enough how good I feel and how bad I can finally leave in the past.

I wrote this for me as much as I did you, but more for my kids who had to deal with a phase of my life—*their lives*—that paralleled my dad's, where I was absentee, living an adventure on a mountain, changing lives without making the lives of my kids and my family a better for it. I wrote this because another cycle has been broken, a cycle of sorrow that began in 1988 and ended on December 17, 2022. I think that cycle's gone for good.

No. I know the cycle's ended. This will be—this is—my last visit to The House on West Grand.

Tomorrow is a new day.

ACKNOWLEDGMENTS

For everyone whose help made this story possible:

Thank you to my wife, Valeria. Your motivation kept me writing when parts of this story made me want to stop. You're the love of my life, my best friend, and everything I could ever ask for.

Thank you, Ashley. Again, your support for this work and its fruition is invaluable.

Erik McDaniel, thank you for your input and ever-scrutinizing gaze on my work. Trinity Rose, thank you for reading my first draft (and using it as a 'scary' bedtime story); thank you for your feedback. It helped so much. Bethany Sparvel, I know you knew some of the story, but thank you for reading and sharing that it had your stomach in knots. What a terrible thing to thank you for, but it at least let me know my work was heading in the right direction.

Thank you, Mom, for your input and experiences with that whited sepulcher that was our family's last attempt at keeping it together, for reminding me of things I'd forgotten, and for revealing that *Dad* was as afraid of the house as the rest of us.

My thanks to my sister, who specifically asked not to be named in this story (I don't blame you), and your input. I'd only known about the bloody Mary, but I didn't remember the thorn bush or that you avoided your room as often as possible, only to find our parent's bed empty.

Thank you, Shawn Stewart. You've stood by me through thick and thin, provided my previous works with a soundtrack, and always been one of my strongest supporters in all my writing endeavors.

Lastly, thank you, "Blue Boy," Mr. Robert Vargas, Junior. I'm thankful we got to be kids together. You've helped me to put this story to rest, finally.

I'm finally free.

Thank you for Reading this Book!

Please take a moment and leave a book review on Amazon, Goodreads, another venue, or (if you are amazing & have the time) multiple sites.

Honest reviews help our books gain visibility to other readers who may be interested, and they are always appreciated by both Madhouse Books and our featured authors.

Please also take a moment to visit Madhouse Books online for information on news and upcoming releases!

MadhouseBooks.com